WILLIAM L. SHIRER

THE RISE & FALL OF ADOLF HITLER

COVER DESIGN BY SHARON WAY

SBS SCHOLASTIC BOOK SERVICES
New York • London • Richmond Hill, Ontario

Copyright © 1961 by William L. Shirer. This Scholastic Book
Services edition is published by arrangement with Random
House.

3rd printing.................................February 1967

Printed in the U.S.A.

CONTENTS

PART 1

THE RISE OF ADOLF HITLER

PART 2

HITLER CONQUERS GERMANY

PART 3

HITLER CONQUERS EUROPE

PART 4

THE FALL OF ADOLF HITLER

PART 1

THE RISE OF ADOLF HITLER

Father and Son

One day when Adolf Hitler was only eleven years old he got into a violent quarrel with his father. The stern and stubborn parent was a retired customs official in Austria. He insisted that his son follow in his footsteps when he grew up. But the boy had already made up his mind that he wanted to be an artist. His father, he later recounted, was struck speechless at such an idea.

"Artist!" exclaimed the father. "No! Never as long as I live!"

Angry words flamed up between them. But the youth would not give in. He refused even to consider becoming a government official. The very idea of sitting in an office filling out forms, he said, made him sick to his stomach. He was determined to become a painter.

Hitler never became a painter, though he considered himself to be an "artist" to the end of his life. But this determined stand against his father at a time when he was only a boy in the sixth grade at school revealed a fierce, unbending will that was to carry him far in this world.

In fact, combined with other qualities, it carried him to a point where he became the dictator of Germany and then the conqueror of most of Europe. As a conqueror he belongs in history with Alexander the Great, Julius Caesar and Napoleon Bonaparte.

Like them he was undoubtedly a genius. But it must be added at once that he was an evil genius, one of the cruelest, most bloodthirsty and barbarous tyrants who ever lived. Perhaps it would be more accurate historically to say that Hitler was closer to Genghis Khan, the ruthless Asiatic conqueror, than to Alexander, Caesar and Napoleon.

Absolute power corrupted him, as it does all who hold it. Before he died at the age of fifty-six he had massacred millions of innocent persons, including some five million Jews. And he had plunged the world into the bloodiest and most destructive war in history.

We know much more about Hitler than we shall ever know about such illustrious predecessors of his as Alexander, Caesar, Napoleon and Genghis Khan. For one thing, he was a child of our time. Millions of persons still living remember him. Many of them suffered from his barbarous acts. For many years my own job, as an American correspondent in Berlin, gave me the opportunity to meet him, to listen to his numerous speeches and to observe him at first hand at the moment of his greatest triumphs.

Furthermore, at the end of World War II in 1945, the victorious Allies captured most of his secret papers. They were found in abandoned mines and in cellars of old castles where they had been hidden by the Germans. We can thus tear away the curtain that for so long hid his odious acts.

We can read his confidential letters. We can follow his secret talks to his generals and see him plotting war and conquest. We can watch him browbeating his victims, double-crossing his friends and enemies, ordering the murder of his opponents and the massacre of the millions he disliked.

Never before in history has there been such a well-documented story as this one. There is no need to invent or to imagine anything, as chroniclers of the lives of great men who lived in the distant past sometimes have done. What is set down in this book is based almost entirely on Hitler's own records, or on what the author saw in Germany with his own eyes.

The story of the life of Adolf Hitler both fascinates and repels one. He rose literally from the gutter to become the greatest conqueror of the twentieth century. He overcame incredible obstacles in his rise to power. What he did with his power—how he abused it—we shall see.

School Days and an Interlude
of Loafing

Adolf Hitler was born April 20, 1889, in a modest inn in the Austrian town of Braunau-on-the-Inn across the border from Germany.

Austria was a part of the Austro-Hungarian Empire, which was ruled by the ancient and autocratic House of Hapsburgs, the oldest ruling family in Europe. This Austro-Hungarian Empire no longer exists. It was destroyed at the end of World War I (which it largely provoked) when the various nationalities that comprised it—the Poles, Czechoslovaks, Hungarians and Yugoslavs—broke away to form their own countries.

But at the time of Hitler's birth, eleven years before the end of the nineteenth century, Austria-

Hungary was one of the most important empires in Europe. It sprawled along the Danube River in central and southeastern Europe. It had a large army and navy. It was economically prosperous. It had an extensive aristocracy made up of dukes, archdukes, princes, counts and barons, most of whom lived in beautiful castles or palaces.

The Austrians, though outnumbered by the other nationalities, dominated the empire. They were a branch of the Germanic people and spoke German. Many, like Hitler, thought of themselves as German. This must be kept in mind in tracing the career of the future German dictator. Though born an Austrian, he considered himself to be as good a German as those who lived in Germany. And he thought that all "Germans" should be united into one country—an objective he ultimately achieved for a short time.

His father, as we have seen, was a stern, short-tempered man. Adolf respected him but did not get along with him. His mother, as he often said later, he loved. She was a gentle, devout woman, devoted to her husband and especially to her children.

Until Adolf came into conflict with his father, he too seems to have been a gentle and devout child. Indeed while attending elementary school at the

Benedictine monastery at Lambach he became a choirboy and dreamed of becoming a Catholic priest.

At this school and at others his grades at first were quite good. But he claimed that his quarrels with his father over what he intended to be when he grew up caused him to lose interest in getting good marks. From the sixth grade on they became progressively worse. At the age of sixteen, when he was midway through secondary school, he became so discouraged that he quit school for good.

Forever after he blamed his teachers for his scholastic failure. "The majority of them," he wrote later when he had grown up, "were somewhat mentally deranged, and quite a few ended their lives as lunatics." To blame others for our failures is a common fault. But Hitler then—and later—carried it to extremes. He was always finding a scapegoat.

One of his teachers, he later admitted, did inspire him in his youth. This was Leopold Poetsch, who taught history at the secondary school. Young Adolf was carried away by his dazzling eloquence.

"You cannot imagine," Hitler once exclaimed years afterward, "how much I owe to that old man!"

Although Adolf was bored by most of the subjects he was forced to take, he developed a passion for history. This was to help him in his ultimate career.

Hitler once described the three years after he quit school as the happiest days of his life. His father had died in the meantime, leaving his mother but a small pension to support herself and her two children, Adolf and a younger sister named Paula.

Adolf refused to get a job or to learn a trade, as most boys did when they quit school. Regular employment disgusted him—not only at the age of sixteen but throughout his life. He never once held a steady job until he became dictator of a great country.

Instead of working and trying to help his mother, he preferred to loaf. So for three years after he left school, from the age of sixteen to nineteen, he spent his time roaming the streets of Linz, a pleasant Austrian town on the Danube River, and dreaming of his future as an artist. Evenings he would often spend at the opera, for he also had a passion for music and especially for the mystic opera music of Richard Wagner, the great German composer.

A ticket for standing room at the opera cost him

no more than the equivalent of ten cents. Nevertheless, attending the opera took most of his meager pocket money. The rest he spent on books, for he also read a great deal. Hours on end he would curl up with books on German history and mythology. He could not, of course, afford to buy these books. He borrowed them from lending libraries, which charged a small fee. There were no free public libraries in Austria in those days.

And he brooded. He became deeply concerned with the ills of the world. His one boyhood friend later recounted: "Hitler was always up against something and at odds with the world. I never saw him taking anything lightly."

This friend has described young Adolf at this period as a pale, sickly, lanky youth who was usually shy and reticent. But he could also fly into sudden bursts of hysterical anger against those who disagreed with him.

We thus see forming in Hitler in his early teens some of the aspects of character and mind which later played a key roll in his life. He was at odds with the world and he angrily resented anyone disagreeing with him.

At eighteen, Hitler received a shattering blow from which he never entirely recovered. He flunked the entrance examination at the Vienna Academy of Fine Arts. His crude, lifeless drawings convinced the teachers who examined him that he would be wasting his time—and theirs—in trying to achieve his great ambition of becoming a painter.

This failure became one of Hitler's major, lifelong frustrations. To the very end of his life he saw himself as an "artist" who had been denied recognition by "stupid" teachers.

Another terrible blow soon followed. The next year his beloved mother died of cancer just four days before the family would have celebrated Christmas. It was a sad Yuletide for the nineteen-year-old youth.

It was a dreadful blow [he wrote later]. I had honored my father, but my mother I had loved. Her death put a sudden end to all my high-flown plans. Poverty and hard reality compelled me to take a quick decision. I was faced with the problem of somehow making my own living.

Somehow! He had no trade. He had always disdained manual or office work. He had never tried to earn a cent. But he was undaunted. Bidding his relatives farewell, he declared that he would never return to his hometown of Linz until he had made good.

With a suitcase full of clothes and underwear in my hand [he later wrote of his departure] and an indomitable will in my heart, I set out for Vienna.

I too hoped to wrest from fate what my father had accomplished fifty years before. I too hoped to become "something"—but in no case a civil servant.

Down and Out in Vienna—
"The Saddest Period of My Life"

The next four years in Vienna, between 1909 and 1913, turned out to be a time of utter misery for Hitler.

This was the period when he was entering manhood—between the ages of twenty and twenty-four. Usually these are happy years. A young man is getting a start in life, and all beginnings are exciting. They bring fresh experiences, new problems and unexpected challenges that stimulate a youth to make the most of himself.

No city on earth was more congenial to get a start in than Vienna, the capital of the old Austro-Hungarian Empire. It was—and is—one of the most beautiful cities of Europe. It lies along the blue

14

Danube River beneath the wooded hills of the Vienna Forest. There is a stately atmosphere about the city, as befits a once imperial capital. It has wide, tree-lined boulevards, spacious parks, elegant public buildings, soaring church spires, and is dotted with many splendid old palaces.

In Hitler's time—as before and afterward—music filled the air. It was the music of the great composers who had lived there—Haydn, Mozart, Beethoven and Schubert—and in the last Indian-summer years of the empire, the gay, haunting waltzes of Vienna's own beloved Johann Strauss.

The Viennese are the most attractive people I have ever known in Europe. They are gay. They find life worth living and they make the most of it. They like music. They like to dance, especially waltzes, which they originated. They like to meet with one another in coffeehouses and have good talk. They go often to the theater and they have a passion for the opera. They enjoy good food and wine. And when the times are difficult they like to dream of a better life.

But Hitler did not share in the gaiety or in the dreams of the Viennese, nor did he appreciate the beauty of the city. His years in Vienna he later called "the saddest period of my life." It is easy to see why.

For one thing, he shunned regular employment. He preferred to putter about at odd jobs: shoveling snow, beating carpets and carrying bags outside a railroad station. Occasionally when he was desperate he worked as a building laborer, but not often for he hated such hard work. Without regular wages he was forced to live in what we would call flophouses. His clothes were shabby, his hair uncut, his face unshaved. He became a vagabond.

Contrary to a popular legend, Hitler was never a paper hanger or a house painter. He was too lazy to acquire those skills. He did eventually earn some money painting crude water-color pictures for posters and advertisements. This satisfied his "artistic" ambitions to some extent, but not the requirements of his stomach.

It was truly a meager living [he wrote later] which never sufficed to appease even my daily hunger.

Hunger was then my faithful bodyguard; he never left me for a moment and partook of all I had. My life was a continuous struggle with this pitiless friend.

Anyone who saw the future German dictator on the streets of Vienna in those days must have thought he was what we Americans would call a bum. He was down and out, and looked it.

And yet there is another side to this story of

his vagabond days in Vienna. Unlike most of the tramps who plodded the streets with him, he neither smoked nor drank. Unlike them, too, he read much. In fact, without much work to do, he spent most of his days and evenings devouring books and pondering them.

From the reading of books and from a firsthand experience of the seamy side of life, Hitler learned during these vagrant early years in Vienna almost all that he was to know throughout his life. He often said so himself.

Vienna [he wrote years afterward] was the hardest, most thorough school of my life. I had set foot in this town while still half a boy, and I left it a man, grown quiet and grave.

In this period there took shape within me a world picture and a philosophy which became the granite foundation of all my acts. In addition to what I then created, I have had to learn little; and I have had to alter nothing.

What, then, did Hitler learn as a down-and-out tramp in Vienna between the ages of twenty and twenty-four? What was the "world picture and philosophy" upon which he later based the awful deeds that nearly destroyed the world? It is of vital importance to know the answers to these questions. They explain a great deal of world history during the third and fourth decades of the twentieth century.

First, Hitler learned to glorify war and conquest. The finest thing men could do, he concluded, was to go to war and conquer foreign peoples. Peace, he decided, was a bad thing for mankind. It corrupted men and made them soft.

What about the millions of men who were killed in wars while still young? And the millions of others who were maimed—blinded for the rest of their lives or crippled by the loss of a leg or an arm? Hitler didn't much care. That was the way life was, he said—hard and cruel.

In his Vienna days Hitler also conceived the preposterous idea that the Germans were superior to all other peoples. They were, he was sure, stronger and more intelligent and more skillful than Americans or Britishers or Italians or Russians or others. In fact to him the Germans were the Master Race. Other people were fit only to be their slaves.

This was a widely held view among Germans in those days. And though Hitler was an Austrian, many Austrians, as we have said, considered themselves as German as the people who lived in Germany.

The young tramp in Vienna also absorbed a

number of political ideas which he later put into practice in Germany. He saw that if a political party were to be successful it had to know how to attract millions of people. It had to master the art of propaganda, which, as he understood it, often meant telling lies to people. He once said that the bigger the lie the better, because it was easier to make people believe a big lie than a small one. Also, he came to believe that a political party must know how to use terror. That meant bashing in the heads of political opponents, or sometimes even killing them.

Finally, Hitler saw the value of oratory in politics. Only a man who could sway the masses of people by his eloquence, he came to believe, could succeed in politics.

The power that has always started the great religious and political avalanches in history rolling [he wrote later] has been the magic of the spoken word, and that alone.

In this matter Hitler practiced what he preached. He became the greatest orator of his time on the continent of Europe. I myself listened to many of his speeches and perceived the magic of his spoken words. I saw him hold huge audiences in his spell. Only Winston Churchill in England was his equal.

In America we had no orator in those days to match Hitler.

It was in Vienna, too, that Hitler developed his grotesque hatred for the Jews. In his book, *My Struggle* (in German it is called *Mein Kampf*), Hitler claimed to remember the very day that, as he says, he became a confirmed anti-Semite—or hater of Jews. He was walking in Vienna when he suddenly encountered a man who looked strange to him because of his long black coat and side whiskers.

"Is this a Jew?" he says was his first thought. "But the longer I stared at this foreign face the more my first question assumed a new form: 'Is this a German?'"

Wherever I went [Hitler continued the story] I began to see Jews, and the more I saw, the more sharply they became distinguished in my eyes from the rest of humanity. I grew sick to the stomach. I began to hate them. I became an anti-Semite.

He was to remain a blind and fanatical one to the end of his life. This prejudice against the Jews became with Hitler a terrible disease which led to the massacre of millions of innocent Jewish men, women and children. Quite a few other Germans were afflicted with this bigotry. But they were mostly unimportant persons. What is significant to this story is that, after Hitler became the German dictator and had the power of life and death over millions of people, he allowed this diseased hatred of the Jews to get the upper hand in him. It drove him to wipe out half of the Jews of Europe.

In the spring of 1913, when he was twenty-four years old, Hitler left Vienna for Munich, in Germany. In his autobiographical book he gives several reasons for this move, but not the most important one. He says he could not stand all the mixture of races in Vienna, especially the presence of "Jews—and more Jews." He says his heart had always been in Germany.

But the principal reason he left Austria was to escape military service. For three years—since his twenty-first birthday—he had dodged it. Not, it appears, because he was a coward, but simply because he loathed serving in the ranks with Jews.

When Hitler arrived in Munich he was still penniless. To everyone except himself he must have seemed a total failure. He had no friends, no family, no home, no job, no prospects.

He had, however, one thing: an unquenchable confidence that he would still make good. Just how, he did not yet know.

The coming of World War I in 1914 offered

Hitler an escape from all the failures and frustrations of his personal life. It came, he later said, "as a deliverance from the distress that had weighed upon me during the days of my youth. I am not ashamed to say that I sank down on my knees and thanked Heaven." He petitioned King Ludwig III of Bavaria for permission to serve in a Bavarian regiment and it was granted.

The war, which would bring death to millions of young men, brought for Adolf Hitler, at twenty-five, a new start in life.

Fateful Decision: Hitler Goes into Politics

Like millions of other Germans, Adolf Hitler proved to be a brave and courageous soldier. Later some of his political opponents charged that he was a coward in combat. But that was not true. He served four years on the Western front in France as a dispatch runner in the First Company of the Sixteenth Bavarian Reserve Infantry Regiment. He was twice wounded and twice decorated for bravery with the Iron Cross. Despite this record his promotion as a soldier was slow. In four years at the front he rose only from private to corporal. What he later believed to be his military genius was not recognized by his superior officers in World War I.

Like millions of other Germans, too, Hitler could not accept Germany's military defeat by Great Britain, France and the United States in 1918. Like them, he embraced the legend that the German army had not been defeated on the battlefield but had been, as they said, "stabbed in the back" by the slackers at home. Hitler was sure that these "slackers" were mostly Jews and "red" pacifists.

Hitler's belief in this fraudulent legend led him to make the crucial decision of his life: to go into politics. We can pinpoint the exact moment of this move.

On the dark, autumn Sunday morning of November 10, 1918, a pastor came bearing unbelievable news for the wounded soldiers in a military hospital near Berlin. Among the soldiers was Hitler, who was recovering from temporary blindness suffered in a British gas attack a month before.

Kaiser Wilhelm II, the emperor of Germany, had abdicated and fled to neutral Holland, the pastor told them. A republic had been proclaimed in Berlin. On the following day, the pastor said, the German army would surrender to the Allies at Compiègne, in France. The war was lost. The pastor began to sob. So did the blinded Corporal Hitler.

> I could stand it no longer [Hitler later recounted]. I groped my way back to the ward, threw myself on my bunk and dug my burning head into my pillow.
>
> So it had been in vain . . . the two million dead. Had they died for this? So that a gang of wretched criminals could lay hands on the Fatherland?

There followed for him, Hitler later said, "terrible days and even worse nights. . . . Hatred grew in me for those responsible for this deed. Miserable and degenerate criminals!"

And then, he recalled, "my own fate became known to me. I decided to go into politics." This turned out to be a fateful decision—not only for Adolf Hitler but also for the world.

The prospects for a political career in Germany for this twenty-nine-year-old Austrian, without friends or funds, were less than promising. Returning to civilian life, he had no trade or profession by which to earn a living. He had little schooling and no experience whatsoever in politics.

For a brief moment he realized how bleak his prospects were. "Nameless as I was, I did not possess," he wrote later, "the least basis for any useful political action." Nevertheless he had an immense confidence in himself. He was sure an opportunity would appear, and soon it did.

Not wishing at twenty-nine, any more than when he was twenty, to get a steady job in civilian life, he contrived to stay on in the army. Here at least he was fed and clothed and given shelter. He was posted at Munich, which he now regarded as his second home. His assignment in the army was to spy on political parties which the defeated German generals suspected might be "subversive" —that is, communist or socialist or pacifist.

One day in September, 1919, Hitler received an order to take a look at a small political group in Munich that called itself the German Workers' party. The generals were suspicious of all parties of workingmen.

He found a gathering of about twenty-five people in the back room of a beer hall. Hitler discerned nothing subversive about them. But neither did he see anything of importance about them. When the next day he received an invitation to join this tiny political party he says he "didn't know whether to be angry or to laugh."

And yet . . . there was something about the

shabby men that attracted the man who had once been a down-and-out tramp in Vienna. They were his kind of people. Back in the army barracks he found himself facing what later he called "the hardest question of my life: should I join?" And then, he later wrote:

After two days of agonized pondering and reflection, I finally came to the conviction that I had to take this step. It was the most decisive resolve of my life.

Adolf Hitler was thereupon enrolled as the seventh member of the Committee of the German Workers' party. It was from this small and insignificant organization that Hitler fashioned the Nazi Party and eventually made it by far the largest political party in Germany, with millions of enthusiastic members.

How did he do it, he who had always shunned hard, regular work? To the surprise of all who had come into contact with him, Hitler suddenly revealed a ferocious energy and drive. All the warped ideas which had been bubbling in his strange mind since the lonesome days of hunger in Vienna now found an outlet.

He soon proved to be a brilliant organizer and

a shrewd propagandist. By what can only be termed an evil stroke of genius, he gave the Nazi movement a flag, a symbol, in the form of the ancient swastika cross. This hooked cross was to many the sign of Aryan (that is, non-Jewish) purity and supremacy. It soon took on a strange fascination for numbers of Germans, who flocked under its banner.

Hitler founded a party army of so-called storm troopers, the *Sturmabteilung*, which became widely known as the "S.A." Its brown-shirted toughs soon spread terror among Hitler's political opponents. They broke up their meetings, gave them beatings and sometimes murdered them.

And perhaps most important of all, Hitler soon became a dazzling orator. During his vagabond days in Vienna he had perceived that all great political movements were sparked by "the magic of the spoken word, and by that alone." But for years he did not know whether he himself had the makings of a great public speaker. He had no opportunity to put himself to the test.

One day in Munich, not long after joining the party, he got his big chance. He was scheduled to make a brief preliminary speech at a political rally of the German Workers' party. The main address was to be given by the party's president, who did not think much of his subordinate's oratory.

Hitler stole the show! "I spoke for thirty minutes," he later wrote. "And what previously I had simply felt within me was now proved by reality. I could speak!" From then on he drew large audiences. Many came just to hear him orate. They often left the hall converted to nazism.

By 1921, only two years after he joined the party as a "nameless" follower, Hitler had succeeded by shrewdness, ruthlessness and his prowess as a spellbinder in making himself absolute dictator of it. He changed the name of the party to the "National Socialist German Workers' party." (The term *Nazi* is an abbreviation of the first part of the German name for the party—*Nationalsozialist-ische*.) He assumed the title of *Führer,* or Leader. Everyone else in the party was subordinate to him.

These subordinate leaders who helped Hitler on the road to political power in Germany were an odd assortment. They included Captain Ernst Roehm, a tough, scar-faced professional army officer, and Hermann Goering, a famous fighter pilot during World War I and a drug addict. There was Dietrich Eckart, a drunken poet who had once been confined in a mental institution, and Rudolf

Hess, a starry-eyed student at the University of Munich. There was Alfred Rosenberg, a confused Balt, who in 1917 had graduated from the University of Moscow and had nearly become a Russian Bolshevik before emigrating to Munich to become a German Nazi.

There was Gregor Strasser, a druggist, who became the number two man in the party; and Strasser's secretary, a bespectacled chicken farmer by the name of Heinrich Himmler. The latter rose to be head of the black-coated S.S., chief of the secret police (Gestapo) and one of the most sinister and powerful men in Europe. Julius Streicher was another early Nazi leader. A former schoolteacher, he soon earned the name of "the Jew-baiter of Nuremberg." I used to see him striding the streets of that ancient town brandishing a whip, which he used freely on Jews. Another important aide to Hitler in later years was Joseph Goebbels, a brilliant but deceitful propagandist and orator. At the beginning of the 1920's he was still a university student.

Such were the principal misfits who helped Adolf Hitler, himself a misfit, conquer Germany.

By the autumn of 1923 Hitler believed himself strong enough to attempt that conquest. He plotted to stage a revolt in Munich and bring down the

German Republic, after which he would make himself dictator of Germany.

This first attempt to seize political power became known in history as Hitler's Beer Hall Putsch. It is a strange story.

The Beer Hall Putsch

History teaches us that no serious political revolution can have much chance of success unless the mass of people are ready for it. If they are miserable enough and desperate enough they may welcome a revolution whose leaders promise a way out of their troubles.

Toward the end of 1924 Adolf Hitler believed that events were ripe for an attempt to overthrow the German Republic. The fledgling Republic was only five years old, yet it seemed to be floundering. Politically, economically and socially Germany was in a mess. At the beginning of the year the French army had occupied the Ruhr, the industrial heart of Germany, because the German government had failed to meet its reparation payments called for under the Treaty of Versailles. The mines and the factories of the Ruhr, on which the life of Germany depended, had closed down. Millions of men were thrown out of work. Business was at a standstill.

But that was not all. German currency had ceased to have any value. The mark had originally been worth twenty-five cents. By November, 1923, it had dropped to a rate of four billion marks to the dollar. This meant that forty million marks were worth only one cent. The consequences were disastrous. The life savings of every family in the country were wiped out. Their salaries and wages had almost no purchasing power. They could scarcely buy enough food to keep a family alive.

No wonder that the German people were looking for someone to lead them out of this impossible situation. Adolf Hitler, always a supreme egotist, had no difficulty in convincing himself that he was the man to do it. Actually he was overestimating himself. His Nazi party was strong only in the state of Bavaria. Elsewhere in Germany it did not even exist, and in most of the country he was still unknown. Nevertheless, at the beginning of November, 1923, he decided to make his bid for the dictatorship of Germany.

On the evening of November 8, the thirty-four-year-old Nazi chief led his armed storm troopers into the Buergerbräukeller, a large beer hall on the outskirts of Munich. A political rally attended by three thousand supporters of the Bavarian government had already begun. It had been organized by three men who governed Bavaria: Gustav von Kahr, the state commissioner; General Otto von Lossow, the commander of the German armed forces in Bavaria; and Colonel Hans von Seisser, the head of the Bavarian state police.

Kahr was in the middle of his speech when a revolver shot was heard in the hall. Hitler had jumped up on a table and to attract attention had fired his pistol at the ceiling. Kahr paused in his address to see what the commotion was all about. He soon learned.

Hitler, surrounded by a squad of storm troopers brandishing rifles and revolvers, pushed his way to the platform and shoved Kahr aside.

"The national revolution," Hitler shouted, "has begun!"

Next he herded the three government leaders into a small room off stage. Knowing that boldness is half the game in such situations, he pointed his revolver at them and commanded them to join his revolution.

Hitler was realist enough to know that he did

not possess the armed strength to defeat the German army troops and the Bavarian police. His strategy was not to beat them, but to win them over to his side by threats. A loaded pistol can be quite convincing. But it did not convince Kahr, General von Lossow and Colonel von Seisser. They refused to be intimidated. They declined to join Hitler's revolution.

In almost all crises of his life, Hitler showed a remarkable capacity for quick, cool thinking that outwitted his opponents. He showed it now.

Leaving the three stubborn government leaders in the room under armed guard, he dashed back to the hall and announced to the crowd that Kahr, Lossow and Seisser—the Bavarian triumvirate, as they were called—had joined him in forming a new national government for Germany. He himself, he said, would lead the government. General Erich Ludendorff, second only to Field Marshal von Hindenburg as a great hero of World War I, would become commander in chief of the new German army.

The big lie—or rather, the two big lies—worked.

The Bavarian triumvirate had not joined Hitler. Kahr, Lossow and Seisser were still locked up off stage for refusing to join him. But the crowd did not know this. The people applauded wildly. As for

General Ludendorff, he knew nothing of the revolt and was not present.

But Hitler had sent for him. This was his ace in the hole. For some time the brash young politician had been cultivating the famous general of the old imperial army. Like most of the other generals and like Hitler, General Ludendorff despised the democratic Republic. Hitler's name meant nothing to the Germans outside of Bavaria. But Ludendorff's carried tremendous weight throughout the country.

The timely arrival of Ludendorff saved Hitler—for the time being. Though the General was furious with Hitler for launching a revolution without consulting him—and in a beer hall at that!—he offered to join it. He quickly won over Kahr, Lossow and Seisser, or thought he did. The three men were released and led back to the platform in triumph by Hitler. All five men made brief speeches and swore to support the new revolutionary government.

But proclaiming a revolution is only the first step, and that was as far as Hitler got. He had neglected to occupy the strategic centers of the city, which is really the first thing to do in a revolution. Not even the telegraph office was seized. Over its wires the news of the *Putsch* (as the uprising was called in German) was flashed to Berlin.

Orders from the capital came back immediately to suppress it.

Kahr, Lossow and Seisser needed no urging. They slipped out of the beer hall and gathered their forces—the troops and the police—to put down the rebellion. They proclaimed that the promises extorted from them at the point of Hitler's pistol were null and void. They ordered the Nazi party dissolved.

By dawn of November 9 Hitler realized that he had lost. He had planned to make a revolution *with* the army and police, not *against* them. He proposed to Ludendorff that they retire to the countryside.

The venerable general refused to retreat. He insisted that they march with their storm troopers to the center of Munich, take over the city and proclaim it the capital of the new revolutionary government. Ludendorff was confident that neither the troops nor the police would dare to oppose a war hero such as he was. Reluctantly Hitler agreed to go along.

Shortly after noon on November 9 the ragged column of storm troopers, with Ludendorff, Hitler and Goering in the lead, reached a narrow street in the center of Munich. There a detachment of police, about a hundred strong and armed with rifles, barred the way.

Which side fired first was never established. One eyewitness later testified that Hitler opened fire with his revolver when the police officer in charge refused to obey his order to surrender. At any rate, firing broke out. Within sixty seconds, sixteen Nazis and three policemen lay dead or dying. The rest of the revolutionists, including Adolf Hitler, lay clutching the pavement to save their lives.

All the rest except Ludendorff. He marched proudly between the muzzles of the police rifles until he reached the square beyond. He must have looked a lonely figure. Not one Nazi followed him—not even the Führer, Adolf Hitler.

The future dictator of Germany was, in fact, the first to scamper to safety. Unmindful of the comrades dead and dying (Goering lay on the pavement seriously wounded) Hitler picked himself up, leaped into a waiting car, and was driven to the country home of a Nazi, where he hid out for several days from the police.

To most people in Germany, this seemed to be the end of Hitler and Nazism. The Nazi party was dissolved. Its leaders were arrested for high treason. Its top man, who had run away at the first hail of bullets, seemed utterly discredited. His meteoric political career appeared to be finished.

As things turned out, it had only begun.

By a dazzling display of oratory, Hitler contrived to turn his trial for treason into a public platform from which he established himself for the first time as a national figure. In the eyes of millions of Germans who hated the Republic, he emerged as a patriot and hero. He acted as his own lawyer. And no one else in the courtroom could match his eloquence or his shrewdness in cross-examination. He completely dominated the trial—and the headlines in the world press.

Hitler was found guilty of high treason and sentenced on April 1, 1924, to five years' imprisonment in the fortress of Landsberg. There he was treated as an honored guest and given a comfortable room of his own with a splendid view over the orchards of the adjoining countryside.

In such pleasant surroundings, the prisoner settled down to ponder his mistakes, to take stock of the future—dismal as that future seemed—and to dictate the text of a book.

Into this book the fallen Nazi leader began to pour the burning thoughts which were to shape the course of German history for the next two decades. He began to set down in detail the blueprint for the kind of Germany—and Europe—he intended to establish when destiny again called, as he was certain it would.

It was not Hitler's fault if the men who ruled the democratic German Republic and the statesmen who presided over the governments of the other countries in Europe did not read his book when it was published. Or, if they read it, did not take it seriously.

No one can say that Adolf Hitler did not give full warning of the barbarian world he intended to make.

PART 2

HITLER CONQUERS GERMANY

A Revealing Book and a New Start

Adolf Hitler was released from Landsberg Prison five days before Christmas in 1924. Thanks to a Yuletide amnesty, he had had to serve less than a year of his five-year sentence for high treason. Though happy to be out of prison, he faced a bleak Christmas. His prospects seemed utterly hopeless.

The Nazi party, which he had built up from nothing, was banned. He himself was forbidden to speak in public. He was threatened with deportation from Germany to his native Austria.

It seemed to almost everyone in Germany that Hitler was finished. Even most of his stanchest supporters thought so. Foreign ambassadors in Berlin reported confidently to their governments that the flamboyant Nazi leader would soon be a forgotten man. To the millions of Germans who supported the democratic Republic, Hitler had turned out to be that worst of all failures—a joke. They still laughed when they recalled the comic-opera Beer Hall Putsch. They made fun of Hitler's "toothbrush" mustache, which resembled the one made famous by the great movie comedian, Charlie Chaplin.

But it was Hitler who eventually had the last laugh. He was not, as we have seen, a man who was easily discouraged. He picked up the threads of his life in his shabby two-room apartment in a run-down section of Munich. The contemplation of his misfortunes only strengthened his conviction that he had a great mission to perform. All great men, he said to himself, had their setbacks. Overcoming them only proved one's greatness.

In this spirit of renewed self-confidence he finished dictating the book he had begun in prison. He set down on paper for all to ponder the blueprint of what he believed the Almighty had called upon him to do in this world and the perverted philosophy that would sustain it.

Hitler wanted to call his book *Four and a Half Years of Struggle against Lies, Stupidity and Cowardice*. But Max Amann, who had been his top sergeant during the war and was now manager of the Nazi publishing business, rebelled. Such a long and ponderous title would never sell. He insisted on shortening it to *My Struggle—Mein Kampf*.

It became one of the most influential books of a demented age, and eventually it outsold all other books in Germany except the Bible. By 1933 its royalties had made author Hitler a millionaire.

In substance, *My Struggle* is an expansion of the half-baked ideas which Hitler picked up during his vagabond days in Vienna. These ideas had been matured by his experience as a soldier in World War I. Hitler brought them up to date and applied them to Germany's problems in the troubled 1920's. Let us try to sum them up.

Germany's first task, Hitler declared, was to recover from the humiliating defeat of 1918. He urged tearing up the Versailles Treaty, which the victorious Allies had imposed on the Germans after the war. This would free Germany from paying reparations and it would free her to rearm. Once Germany had a big army and navy again, she would become "lord of the earth." Those are Hitler's very words. He wanted Germany to become master of the world.

How could it reach this exalted position?

First, Hitler proposed, there must be a "final

reckoning with France, the mortal enemy of the German people." France, he declared, must be destroyed.

Then, with its rear in the West protected, Germany could turn to conquests in the East. The first targets would be those countries with large German minorities. These were his native Austria, and Czechoslovakia and Poland. After them would come the big prize.

The big prize was Russia. In his book, Hitler was quite frank about it. "If we speak of soil in Europe to conquer," he wrote, "we can have primarily in mind only Russia. This soil exists for the people which possesses the force to take it."

He did not think it would be difficult for Germany to take Russia. The Soviet Union, he said, was "ripe for collapse."

Can anyone contend that Hitler's plans for the future—for a new world war—were not clear and precise? He would destroy France and then conquer the East.

During the later years when I was working in Berlin, I watched Hitler take one country after another. I used to wonder why the world was so surprised at this tyrant doing exactly what he had said in his book he would do. But until it was too late, few people believed him.

Not even Hitler's fellow Germans believed him. His book gave full warning of what he would do to Germany if he came to power. He would, he boasted, destroy the Republic, abolish democracy, stamp out the workers' free trade unions and establish himself as supreme dictator. Also, he added, he would "settle" with the Jews.

Finally, Hitler's book was studded with gems of that warped philosophy which he had picked up as a tramp—though a well-read one—in Vienna. Unfortunately it was a philosophy which some of Germany's most learned philosophers had taught during the nineteenth century. Hitler picked it up from reading them.

To us today such a philosophy seems utterly outlandish. But many Germans in Hitler's time took it seriously. Consider a few typical examples from the Nazi leader's book.

Mankind has grown great in eternal struggle, and only in eternal peace does it perish. . . .
Nature confers the Master's right on the strongest. They must dominate. They have the right to victory.
Those who do not want to fight in this world do not deserve to live. Even if this were hard—that is how it is!

With such barbaric ideas buzzing in his head, Hitler set out to rebuild the Nazi party and to plot new strategy and tactics for the conquest of Germany. The failure of the Beer Hall Putsch had taught him one lesson. There must be no further attempt at armed revolt.

Henceforth, he decided, the Nazi party would depend on votes to sweep it into power in Berlin. "We shall have to hold our noses and enter the Reichstag," he told one of his cronies. The Reichstag was the popularly elected legislative body of Germany, equivalent to our House of Representatives.

Two weeks after his release from prison Hitler promised the state government of Bavaria that if it lifted the ban on the Nazis, the party would restrict itself to going after votes in a peaceful, democratic manner. The ban was lifted. But Hitler did not keep his word for long.

On February 27, 1925, he addressed the first mass meeting of the reborn Nazi party at the Buergerbräukeller. This was the big beer hall which he and his followers had last seen on the morning they set out on their ill-fated march to take over Munich and overthrow the Republic.

Carried away by the enthusiasm of the crowd and by his own eloquence, Hitler threatened the state with a new wave of Nazi violence. The Bavarian government promptly forbade him to speak again in public. The ban was also applied by the other states in Germany and lasted two years.

This was a heavy blow to a man whose brilliant oratory had brought him so far. A silenced Hitler was a defeated Hitler. Or so most people in Germany thought.

But again they were wrong. They forgot that Hitler was an organizer as well as a spellbinder. Curbing his resentment at being forbidden to make speeches, the Nazi chief set to work with furious energy to make the Nazi party a political organization such as Germany had never known. It would be, he decided, like the army—a state within a state. That would make it all the easier to take over the nation when the time came.

"We recognized," Hitler said later of this period, "that it is not enough to overthrow the old state. A new state must previously have been built up."

And that is what he did.

Progress was slow at first. Prosperity had finally come to Germany in 1925, as it had to all of the Western world. With better times there was a general feeling of relaxation after so many years of war and turmoil and hunger.

This was not the kind of soil in which a revolutionary movement such as nazism could thrive. By the end of 1925, Hitler had attracted only twenty-seven thousand dues-paying party members. By the end of 1928, after four years of hard work, the membership had risen by four times. But in the national elections that year the Nazis polled fewer than one million votes out of thirty-one million cast. They elected only 12 of the Reichstag's 491 members.

The period from 1925 until the coming of the world-wide depression in 1929 was thus a lean one for Hitler politically, though he never lost hope of eventual victory. But so far as his private life was concerned these years, as he later said, were among the best of his life.

For the first and last time, he fell deeply in love.

Hitler Falls in Love

In the summer of 1928 Hitler persuaded his widowed half sister, Frau Angela Raubal, to come from Vienna to keep house for him in the first decent home he could call his own. This woman was the daughter of Hitler's father by an earlier marriage. Six years older than Adolf she had left home when he was still a youth. She had eventually married and perhaps because she was busy raising children of her own had not seen much of her half brother.

He had rented a villa on the Obersalzberg, a mountain ridge above the town of Berchtesgaden in the Bavarian Alps. This is one of the most beautiful spots in Europe, and Hitler came to love it all the rest of the days of his life. The mountain scenery, broken by green valleys, is superb.

Hitler also had practical reasons for making this mountain paradise his country home. It was only three hours by car or train from Munich, the headquarters of the Nazi party. It was even nearer the Austrian border. In fact Hitler had only to climb a nearby mountain, as he sometimes did, to be able to see his native land.

Probably one reason Hitler chose this location was that in case of trouble with the German authorities, he could slip over the mountains to Austria. He had renounced his Austrian citizenship in 1925, shortly after getting out of prison. But he had been unable to obtain German citizenship. He was, in effect, a man without a country. He was thus ineligible to run for public office. This was somewhat of a handicap to the leader of a growing political party in Germany. And until he overcame this drawback he lived in fear of being deported from Germany as an undesirable alien. To avoid arrest and deportation it was convenient to have a home from which he could easily flee over the border.

Frau Raubal, a fine-looking woman and an excellent cook and housekeeper, arrived that summer at Obersalzberg with her two daughters, Friedl and Geli.

Geli was twenty years old. She had flowing blond hair, handsome features, a pleasant voice and a sunny disposition.

Adolf Hitler fell in love with her.

Since her mother was Hitler's half sister, Geli was his niece—or half niece. And he was the young girl's uncle—or half uncle. But that made no difference to the thirty-nine-year-old moon-struck man who had never known true love for a woman before.

He took her everywhere—to meetings and conferences, on long walks in the mountains and to the cafés and theaters in Munich. They became inseparable, and this caused gossip. Even some of the Nazi leaders objected.

Such objections made the Nazi Führer furious. His private life, he said, was his own business. There was no doubt in his mind that this was the one great love of his life—as indeed it was.

Geli's feelings are more difficult to know. She was flattered by the attention of a man now becoming famous. She enjoyed his company. But whether she truly loved him is doubtful. In the end she most certainly did not. Some deep rift grew between them. Its exact nature remains a mystery to this day.

A few facts are known. Each was jealous of the other. Hitler scarcely allowed Geli to have any life of her own. For example, she wished to return to Vienna for a time in order to continue her singing lessons. She had an ambition of her own—to have a career in operetta, the light opera for which Vienna is so famous. Hitler forbade her to go.

Over this and other differences they began to quarrel. Their squabbles became bitter and even violent as the months passed. Hitler had a hot temper and grew hysterically angry at anyone who crossed him. And Geli had a mind and a will of her own.

At the end of the summer of 1931, their three-year romance came to a crisis—and to tragedy. Geli announced that she was returning to Vienna to resume her voice studies. Hitler refused to allow her to go. There was a scene between them in public. Neighbors witnessed it. When Hitler left their Munich apartment on September 17, 1931, to go to Hamburg, Geli cried out from the window as he was getting into his car:

"Then you won't let me go to Vienna?"

"No!" Hitler shouted back.

The next morning Geli Raubal was found shot

dead in her room. The state's attorney, after a thorough investigation, found that it was suicide. The coroner reported that a bullet had gone through her chest below the left shoulder and penetrated the heart. It seemed beyond doubt that she had killed herself. Her uncle had made her so unhappy that she preferred death to life.

Hitler himself was struck down with grief. His friends remained constantly at his side during the following days and nights in order to prevent him from taking his own life. A week after Geli's burial in Vienna, Hitler obtained special permission from the Austrian government to go there. He spent an evening weeping at the grave. For months he was inconsolable.

From this personal blow stemmed an act of self-denial. Already an abstainer from alcohol and tobacco, Hitler resolved never again to eat meat. He became a vegetarian.

To those few persons really close to him, he declared afterward that Geli Raubal was the only woman he ever loved. He always spoke of her with the deepest reverence—and often in tears. Her room in the villa at Obersalzberg remained as she had left it, even when the house was enlarged later. To his dying day, Geli's portrait hung in his bedroom there.

For a brutal, cynical man who seemed to be incapable of loving any other human being, this passion of Hitler's for the youthful Geli Raubal stands out as one of the mysteries of his life. He never again fell seriously in love. Nor did he again contemplate marriage until the day before he died.

Hitler's Drive for Political Power

The world-wide depression which began with the Wall Street crash in 1929 gave Adolf Hitler the opportunity he had been waiting for.

The economic life of the West became paralyzed. Banks failed. Business firms went under. Trade came to a stop. Millions of persons were thrown out of work. Though there was plenty of food available, millions of families found themselves without the money to buy it. There was hunger, chaos, confusion, despair. True, a similar situation prevailed in most countries, including the United States. But it was perhaps worst of all in Germany.

This was just what Hitler needed. What was misery for others was a godsend to him. Only when men were hungry and desperate and businessmen and bankers were going broke could nazism make an appeal to them. Hitler saw that the time for a new drive for political power had come.

His first great opportunity came in the fall of 1930. The strain of the depression was causing democratic, parliamentary government in Germany to break down. The moderate Chancellor, Heinrich Bruening, was forced to rule by presidential decree because the Reichstag refused to vote his emergency measures to stem the tide. Bruening called a national election for September 14, 1930. He hoped to win a stable democratic majority.

His hopes were blasted by Hitler. The Nazi leader, in a whirlwind electoral campaign, promised the German people a way out of their misery. A Nazi government, he declared, would refuse to pay reparations. In fact it would tear up the Versailles Treaty. And, Hitler promised, it would put business back on its feet and see that every German had a job.

Millions of confused, desperate Germans were deceived by this propaganda. The Nazi had received only eight hundred and ten thousand votes two years before. Now they polled six and a half million. Against the twelve seats they previously held in the Reichstag they won one hundred and seven places. Overnight they jumped from the ninth and smallest political party in Germany to the second largest.

This smashing success emboldened Hitler. Less than two years later in the spring of 1932, he decided to run for president against the eighty-four-year-old Field Marshal Paul von Hindenburg, who was up for re-election. Hindenburg, who had commanded the German army in World War I, was a national hero. Yet the brash young Nazi felt confident he could defeat him.

Actually Hitler was not legally eligible to run for president in Germany. As we have seen, he was not a German citizen. But he easily surmounted this obstacle by trickery. On February 25, 1932, the Minister of the Interior (a Nazi) of the small state of Brunswick formally appointed Hitler attaché of the legation of Brunswick in Berlin. No one in Germany had remembered that Brunswick had a "legation" in Berlin. Foreign countries maintained legations in the capital. But the Brunswick "legation" was a joke. However, the joke was on the German people, not on Hitler. By becoming an "attaché," he automatically became a German citizen. He could run for president.

Hitler's bid for the big prize failed. Though he more than doubled the previous record-breaking Nazi poll and received thirteen and a half million votes, this was only thirty-seven per cent of the total. Hindenburg was re-elected with a fifty-three per cent majority—ten per cent of the votes going to a Communist candidate.

The majority of the Germans still rejected Hitler. He tried again to win over that majority in two Reichstag elections later during the year 1932. In the first the Nazis polled nearly fourteen million votes. This entitled them to two hundred and thirty members in Parliament and made them easily the largest party in the country—but still in the minority. In the second election the party's vote declined by two million, and the Nazis lost thirty-four seats in the Reichstag.

The legend that Hitler and the Nazis could not be stopped was shattered. The tide had begun to ebb. It seemed obvious that Hitler could never get a clear majority in free elections.

But were there not other paths to political power? Hitler pondered the question as the year 1932 faded out. The democratic German Republic seemed doomed. The only question was which antidemocratic force would grab control of the country. The Communists were too weak. Hitler realized that the old-school reactionaries—chiefly the Prussian aristocracy, big business and the army —had the inside track. He shrewdly decided to seek their support.

These reactionary groups, by means of various intrigues, had in fact already seized control of the Republic before the end of 1932. In May of that year they had persuaded President von Hindenburg to dismiss Bruening as chancellor and appoint Franz von Papen. The latter was a former army officer of shallow mind who was rejected even by his own party, the Catholic Center party. Finding no support in the Reichstag, Papen was maneuvered out of office on December 1, 1932, by an army general, Kurt von Schleicher.

In spite of their differences, Papen and Schleicher had one purpose in common. They intended to bury the German Republic and eventually restore the Hohenzollern monarchy. This would have meant the end of Hitler and his aspirations to become dictator. Hitler realized this clearly. The time had come, he saw, to do a little intriguing of his own with the reactionaries. But first he had to overcome a crisis in his own party which threatened to become disastrous.

Gregor Strasser, the number two man in the party, had come to the conclusion after the Nazi setback in the November elections that Hitler could never get the majority vote which would make him chancellor. In December, 1932, he therefore urged Hitler to accept an offer from Chancellor Schleicher to become vice-chancellor. Hitler was furious at the very idea. He would not be second man.

The two top Nazi leaders had a showdown meeting in Berlin on December 7. It degenerated into a bitter quarrel that threatened to wreck the party. Hitler was out of his mind, as an entry in the diary of Dr. Goebbels, who was present, makes clear.

For hours the Führer paces up and down in the hotel room. He is embittered. Finally, he stops and says: "If the party falls to pieces, I'll put an end to it all in three minutes with a pistol shot."

The Nazi party did not fall apart and Hitler did not shoot himself. Strasser, who had been boss of the actual party machine, might have achieved both these ends and thus radically changed the course of history. But at the crucial moment he resigned from the party in disgust and went off for a rest in Italy.

Hitler, always at his best when he detected weakness in an opponent, struck swiftly and hard. He took over direction of the party machine himself and purged it of Strasser's supporters. He made all the party bosses sign a new oath of loyalty to himself and acknowledge him as absolute party dictator.

Having re-established his authority within the Nazi ranks, he was ready to renew his bid for political power in Germany. To achieve this, he said frankly, he was quite willing to make a pact with the devil. The devil turned out to be Papen, who was eager for revenge against General Schleicher for having replaced him as chancellor. Papen, as Hitler knew, was still the favorite of President von Hindenburg, who in the absence of any party majority in the Reichstag, appointed whomever he wished to be chancellor.

Papen and Hitler met secretly on January 4, 1933, and worked out a deal. They agreed to form a government in which Hitler would be chancellor and Papen vice-chancellor. In return for being top man, Hitler agreed to appoint a cabinet in which the non-Nazi reactionaries behind Papen would be in the majority. Now all depended on whether the two intriguers could persuade President von Hindenburg to approve their deal.

They worked on the President's son, Colonel Oskar von Hindenburg, and they worked on the aging Field Marshal himself. They also sought and won support from some of the army generals, from the Prussian aristocrats and from leading businessmen and bankers.

Shortly before noon on January 30, 1933, Adolf Hitler was summoned to the Chancellery by President von Hindenburg. Across the square from the Chancellery three men stood at the window in a room at the Kaiserhof Hotel. They were Goering, Goebbels and Captain Roehm—the three top Nazi leaders after Hitler. Roehm focused binoculars on the Chancellery door. He would be able to see from Hitler's face, as Goebbels later said, whether the "miracle" had happened.

A few minutes past noon they saw that it had. Hitler emerged, crying with joy. His eyes, Goebbels noted, were "full of tears."

By means of a shabby political deal with the reactionaries he privately detested—and who despised him—the one-time Vienna tramp and self-styled revolutionary had become chancellor of the German Republic he had sworn to destroy.

Führer and Dictator

It took Adolf Hitler just a year and a half to become absolute dictator of Germany.

At the beginning of 1933 he was merely chancellor. According to the Constitution of the Republic, his term of office depended on his ability to gain and retain the support of the majority of members in the Reichstag. If that majority voted against him he was out as chancellor. President von Hindenburg could also dismiss him.

He faced another handicap, or so it seemed. The Nazis were in a decided minority in the new government. They had only three of the eleven posts in his cabinet. The rest were held by Vice-Chancellor von Papen and his non-Nazi conservative friends. With a majority of eight to three in the cabinet, they were confident that they had Hitler in their pockets. They were soon to be disillusioned.

Within eighteen months they were all eliminated. Their political parties—as well as all others except the Nazi party—were outlawed. The last vestige of democratic, republican institutions was wiped out.

In that brief time Hitler managed to Nazify Germany from top to bottom. By erasing the historic states, he unified the nation for the first time in history. He abolished freedom of speech and of the press, denied the people the most elemental civil rights, persecuted the Christian churches and hounded the Jews. He ordered the murder of many Germans. He had others carted off to concentration camps where they were beaten and, in many cases, ultimately slaughtered. He also began to arm Germany secretly in defiance of the peace treaty and to prepare for aggressive war.

The monstrous figure of a bloodthirsty, unscrupulous tyrant quickly emerged. And yet the overwhelming majority of the German people eventually came to revere and even to worship him.

This attitude of the Germans puzzled me when I came to live and work in Berlin soon after Hitler came to power. I had thought that all men and women of the Western world valued personal freedom above all else in life. To my surprise I found that few Germans seemed to mind that their individual liberties had been taken away. They seemed unconcerned that so much of their fine culture was being destroyed and replaced by a mindless barbarism. And they seemed strangely unaware how Hitler was tricking them.

This blindness to Nazi trickery was shown by their reaction to the great Reichstag fire on the night of February 27, 1933, just a month after Hitler became chancellor. There seems to be no doubt that the Nazis themselves deliberately set the massive building on fire. Yet they convinced most Germans that the Communists were responsible. And Hitler cunningly used the fire as a pretext to unleash a reign of terror—not only against the Communists but against the decent, democratic anti-Nazi parties.

He had called a new election and he knew that he could not win it fairly and honestly. Citing the Reichstag fire as evidence that his opponents were trying to overthrow the government by force, he induced President von Hindenburg to sign a decree "for the protection of the people and state."

It suspended civil liberties and legalized the Nazi terror in suppressing the rival political parties.

Even then Hitler failed to win a majority of the votes of the German people in the election of March 5, 1933. This incidentally was the last relatively free, democratic election which the country was to have during Hitler's lifetime. Some fifty-six per cent of the electorate voted for the non-Nazi parties.

A little further trickery, however, enabled Hitler to consolidate his power. Toward the end of March he simply eliminated enough opposition members of the Reichstag—and threatened enough others with elimination—to get the necessary two-thirds majority of the lower house to amend the Constitution. By this amendment all legislative functions were transferred from the Reichstag to him personally. He was now legally not only the head of the government of Germany but its supreme legislator. It was he, not the Reichstag, who henceforth would make the laws.

Political parties in Germany obviously had become superfluous. By midsummer of 1933 Hitler had forced all the parties but his own to dissolve. On July 14 he decreed that the Nazis would henceforth constitute the sole political party in Germany. Anyone who tried to start a new party or renew one of the old ones would be jailed.

Now only the aging and somewhat senile President von Hindenburg and the German army remained to contest Hitler's dictatorship, though his own Nazi storm troopers were proving troublesome.

The storm troopers, known as the S.A., numbered two million. Led by Roehm, they were clamoring for the radical Nazi revolution that Hitler had promised. They wanted their leader to throw the conservative non-Nazis out of their jobs in government, in industry, even in the army, and give those jobs to them. In fact, they wanted their organization, the S.A., to constitute the new German army. This was most embarrassing to Hitler.

He bided his time for nearly a year. He was a man who had learned how to wait, however impatiently, when the stakes were high.

Then between June and August, 1934, he struck. In a typically cruel and bloody way he solved the problem of rivals to his dictatorship and of the unruly storm troopers crying for a "second revolution." He was assisted by an act of God.

As that fateful summer of 1934 approached, a feverish tension once again gripped Germany. The brown-shirted storm troopers, with their agitation for a "second revolution," were getting out of hand. They were taking over business establishments. They were making thousands of arbitrary arrests and beating up anyone they pleased. Roehm, their leader, was demanding that Hitler disband the old army led by aristocratic Prussian officers—"old clods," he called them. He insisted that his S.A. form a new "People's Army."

Nothing was further from Hitler's intentions. He was much shrewder and saw much further than Roehm and the other Nazi party fanatics. If he were to carry out his long-term plans to conquer Europe he could do it only with the traditional, highly disciplined, Prussian-officered army. The motley mob of brown-shirted toughs would never do. The S.A. had served its purpose. It had conquered the streets of Germany and helped the party to power. Now it would have to be eased from the picture.

The chiefs of the regular army, with the backing of Hindenburg, were in fact demanding it. Unless Hitler suppressed the S.A., they threatened to overthrow him and set up a military dictatorship.

This was not an idle threat, and Hitler had sense enough to realize it. The army alone possessed the physical power—the guns—to remove him. The aroused generals would have to be appeased. They would, in fact, have to be more than appeased. Hitler would need their active support at that crucial moment, which could not be far off, when the aged President von Hindenburg passed on.

As a matter of fact, the question of the President's successor had now become extremely critical for Hitler. He well knew that Hindenburg, as well as the generals, the Prussian aristocracy and most of the conservatives, wanted the Hohenzollern monarchy to be restored in Germany following his death.

This would have doomed Hitler, for a Hohenzollern emperor would never tolerate Hitler as dictator. Nor would he go along with the barbarism of the Nazis.

Early in April of 1934 Hitler was secretly informed that Hindenburg's health was failing fast. The ruthless Nazi leader thereupon decided on a bold stroke.

He proposed a deal to the generals. If they would back him as Hindenburg's successor, he would put a stop to the clamor for a "second revolution," suppress the S.A. and guarantee that the army (along with the navy and eventually the air force) would be the sole bearer of arms in Nazi

Germany. Moreover, despite the disarmament restrictions of the Versailles Treaty, which limited the army to one hundred thousand men, the navy to a few small vessels and which forbade an air force, Hitler promised to restore the armed forces to the size and grandeur they had known in imperial times.

The generals accepted Hitler's offer. Thus at no real cost to himself the Nazi leader had succeeded in receiving the backing of the army to add the presidency to his chancellorship. This would make him undisputed and absolute dictator of Germany.

On June 30, 1934, Hitler carried out his part of the bargain—and even more! He launched what became known in history as the Nazi Blood Purge. He ordered the summary execution not only of the leaders of the S.A. but of dozens of other persons on whom he wanted to take personal revenge.

He himself hauled Roehm, who was his closest personal friend, out of bed early that morning, drove him to a prison in Munich, and had him murdered in his cell. Gregor Strasser, the former number two man in the Nazi party who had dared to cross Hitler, was arrested in Berlin and murdered in *his* cell. General von Schleicher, the former chancellor whom Hitler had succeeded, was shot down and killed in his home by Nazi thugs, as was his wife.

Franz von Papen, the vice-chancellor, who had arranged for Hitler to become chancellor, barely escaped with his life. His three principal aides were murdered and he himself was placed under house arrest. Gustav von Kahr, who had helped suppress Hitler's Beer Hall Putsch in 1923, was not forgotten by the bloodthirsty Chancellor. A gang of Hitler's Nazi cronies hacked Kahr to pieces with a pickax and threw his remains into a swamp near Munich. Some one thousand persons were massacred on Hitler's orders on this bloody weekend.

In a speech to a cheering Reichstag a few days later, Chancellor Hitler assumed full responsibility for the mass murders. He accused Roehm and his other victims of having conspired to overthrow him, though he offered not one shred of evidence. Hitler's megalomania, his delusions of his own greatness, now burst out for all to see. He told the Reichstag:

If anyone reproaches me and asks why I did not resort to the regular courts of justice, then all I can say is this: in this hour I was responsible for the fate of the German people. I became the Supreme Judge of the German people.

The S.A. was broken, as Hitler had promised the generals, though he permitted a remnant to survive under a colorless, servile leader. The army chiefs were pleased. They did not seem shocked at a massacre without precedent in German history, including the murder of two eminent retired generals. In fact, General Werner von Blomberg, the minister of defense, publicly congratulated Hitler for his bloody deed. So did Field Marshal von Hindenburg, in his capacity as the President of Germany.

Fate intervened a few weeks later to remove the last threat to Hitler's absolute dictatorship. The seemingly indestructible Hindenburg died at the age of eighty-six on August 2, 1934.

Hitler was ready to act. The day before, though it was clearly unconstitutional, he had had his cabinet decree a law combining the offices of President and Chancellor. The title of President was abolished. Hitler gave himself a new one: *Führer and Reich's Chancellor*. As successor to Hindenburg, he also became Commander in Chief of the Armed Forces.

This swift step was accompanied by a typical piece of deceit. Hitler suppressed part of Hindenburg's last will and testament. It had recommended the re-establishment of the Hohenzollern monarchy on the President's death.

Before Hindenburg's body was cold, Hitler exacted from all officers and men of the armed forces a personal oath of allegiance—not to the fatherland, not to the Constitution, but to himself as Führer. He made them swear unconditional obedience to him unto death. Now Hitler need no longer fear that the generals might use the army to overthrow him.

I saw a good deal of the Nazi dictator at this time. One day at the annual Nazi party rally at Nuremberg, where he strutted around like a conquering emperor, he said to some of us "It is wonderful!" We had to admit that for him it was.

Adolf Hitler had come a long way from his hungry days as a tramp in Vienna. At forty-five he had completed his conquest of Germany. He could now set out, as Napoleon had set out a little more than a century before, to conquer Europe.

PART 3

HITLER CONQUERS EUROPE

The Bloodless Conquests

A dolf Hitler's first conquests in Europe were bloodless. They were achieved not by the sword but by diplomacy.

Despite his lack of formal education and of any experience whatsoever in foreign affairs, the Führer, as he was now called, quickly became a master at practicing a diplomacy of deceit, threat and bluff. He fooled the statesmen of Europe as easily as he had hoodwinked his fellow Germans.

The inside story of his amazing triumphs can now be put together. Though he plotted his conquests, both peaceful and bloody, in the strictest secrecy, the details of his plans and of his orders for carrying them out were taken down in writing. They are among the captured German documents on which this biography is largely based. Many of them read like parts of a detective story. The recorded dialogue often sounds as if it had been written by some wildly imaginative playwright. But it is all true and factual. This unique material gives us an intimate picture of Hitler the Conqueror.

Between 1933 and 1935 he began secretly to rearm Germany in defiance of the Versailles Treaty. Then on a spring day in 1935—March 16—he came out into the open. He denounced the military restrictions of the peace treaty and publicly announced that Germany would have a peacetime conscript army of thirty-six divisions. Though he did not say so, he ordered Goering to build up an air force, which the peace treaty had prohibited. He also launched a big building program for the hitherto small navy.

A year later he was ready to make his first big move. On March 7, 1936, he sent units of his new army into the demilitarized zone of the Rhineland on Germany's western border. This was not only a breach of the Versailles Treaty, which had been forced on Germany, but of the later Locarno Treaty, which Germany had freely signed.

Hitler's march into the Rhineland was a daring move. It was pure bluff. The French army, as Hitler well knew, was entitled under the two treaties to throw back the German troops in the Rhineland. And it could easily have done so. It was still the strongest military force in Europe. The new German army was as yet no match for it. Yet the French, restrained by Great Britain, did not move. The two great Western democracies did not want to go to war, even though they could easily have won. They wanted peace at almost any price. Hitler's uncanny intuition had convinced him of this. That is why he took the gamble. Still, he spent a very worried weekend, as he later privately admitted.

"The forty-eight hours after the march into the Rhineland," he conceded afterward, "were the most nerve-racking in my life. If the French had marched into the Rhineland, we would have had to withdraw with our tails between our legs. The military resources at our disposal were wholly inadequate for even a moderate resistance."

Hitler also admitted that, had the French marched, it would have been the end of him and of nazism.

"A retreat on our part," he said, "would have spelt collapse. What saved us was my amazing aplomb."

For once he was telling the truth. This was the

last chance the Western democracies had of stopping Hitler at small cost to themselves. A year later feverish rearmament had made the Germany army and air force strong enough to fight a major war. It was not France and Britain but Hitler who would decide whether there was to be another big European war.

Thanks to the captured German papers, we can pinpoint the exact moment when Hitler actually made his "irrevocable decision," as he called it, to go to war. It was one of the most fateful decisions in modern history.

On the evening of November 5, 1937, the Führer called in his generals and in the greatest secrecy told them he had decided to go to war. Not at the moment, he explained, but by 1943 at the latest. The generals were to get ready for it. In the meantime, he said, the first conquests could be carried out without war—one nation at a time. His native Austria would be taken first; then Czechoslovakia. Merely a threat of war would do the trick. It did.

On the wintry morning of February 12, 1938, Hitler received at his Alpine villa above Berchtesgaden Dr. Kurt von Schuschnigg, the Chancellor of Austria. Schuschnigg had come for what he thought would be a frank and civil discussion of the political differences between the two German-speaking countries.

When the Austrian leader opened the conversation by commenting on the splendid view of the snow-covered Alps, Hitler cut him short.

"We did not gather here," he snapped, "to speak of the fine view or the weather."

Whereupon, the Führer poured on his distinguished guest a torrent of abuse.

You have done everything to avoid a friendly policy [Hitler stormed]. The whole history of Austria is just one uninterrupted act of high treason. I can tell you right now, Herr Schuschnigg, that I am absolutely determined to make an end of all this.

When Schuschnigg attempted to reply that Austria's role in history had been "considerable," Hitler shouted: "Absolutely zero! I am telling you, absolutely zero!"

By this time Hitler was raving like a maniac.

I'm telling you once more that things cannot go on this way! I have a historic mission, and this misson I will fulfill because Providence has destined me to do so! Who is not with me will be crushed!

It was Austria which was to be crushed, as

Schuschnigg now realized. At the close of his harangue Hitler presented the Austrian Chancellor with an ultimatum. He demanded the surrender of Austria within one week to the Austrian Nazis (who were outlawed there). Since Hitler's party followers in Austria were under his thumb, this was equivalent to demanding that the country be turned over to him. Schuschnigg saw this and hesitated.

Herr Schuschnigg [Hitler stormed], you will either sign this [the ultimatum] and fulfill my demands within one week, or I will order my army to march into Austria.

The Chancellor of Austria capitulated and signed.

His surrender, however, did not prevent Hitler from ordering German troops into Austria anyway. Though Schuschnigg appointed Austrian Nazis to key posts in his government, as he had promised, he infuriated the German tyrant by scheduling a plebiscite. The Austrian people were to vote whether they wished to remain "free and independent." Yes or no.

The plebiscite, or voting, never took place. It was to be held on March 13, 1938. Hitler knew what answer the Austrian people would give. They vote to remain free. To forestall this, he sent the German army into Austria on the night of March 11.

I was in Vienna that evening and I saw the gallant little country extinguished—my first but not last such experience. Hitler annexed Austria outright and threw Chancellor Schuschnigg into jail. In fact he kept the Austrian leader imprisoned for seven years, five of them in notorious Nazi concentration camps. It was not until the last days of World War II—to skip ahead—that Schuschnigg was liberated by advancing American troops just as he was about to be murdered by the Nazi secret police.

Hitler's triumphant return to his native land of Austria was a spectacle I shall never forget. He was now afire with his fanatical sense of a God-given mission on this earth. When he arrived at his hometown of Linz, he addressed the delirious citizens there. (He had vowed, it will be remembered, never to return until he had made good.)

When years ago I went forth from this town I bore within me precisely the same profession of faith which today fills my heart. If Providence once called me forth from this town to be the leader of the Reich, it must have charged me with a mission which could only be to restore my beloved homeland to the German Reich.

Hitler's return to Vienna a few days later was sweet revenge on a great city which he felt had rejected him in his youth. He who had once tramped the pavements of the capital as a vagabond, unwashed and empty-bellied, had now assumed the powers of the once mighty Austrian Hapsburg emperors, as in Germany he had taken over those of the Hohenzollern kaisers.

Although I had followed his rise to eminence in Germany, I was taken aback as I listened to him speak to the multitude in Vienna. I could swallow his pose as conqueror but not his boasts that he was the agent of the Lord. The corrupting chemistry of naked power, one could see, was already working on this one-time Viennese tramp. It had happened to all the great conquerors in history, I knew. But it was something to see at first hand.

I believe it was God's will [he told the Viennese] to send a youth from here into the Reich, to raise him to be the leader of the nation so as to enable him to lead his homeland into the Reich.

There is a higher ordering. When Herr Schuschnigg broke his agreement, then in that second I felt the call of Providence. And that which took place was only conceivable as the fulfillment of the wish and the will of this Providence.

In three days the Lord has smitten them!

In the early autumn of 1938 and the following spring, I again saw Hitler practicing his degenerate art of conquering a country by threatening to destroy it with his tanks and planes.

After Austria, his next victim was Czechoslovakia. This was a peaceful, democratic republic which had won its independence from Austria-Hungary after the latter's collapse in 1918. As a first step Hitler demanded—under the threat of invasion—the "return" to Germany of three and a half million so-called Sudeten Germans and the land they lived on under the Czechs. (The Sudetenland, a part of historic Bohemia, had belonged to old Austria, never to Germany.)

Somewhat surprisingly, Hitler easily won the support of Neville Chamberlain, the Prime Minister of Great Britain. Chamberlain was quite willing to sacrifice the life of "a faraway country," as he once called Czechoslovakia, if the peace of Europe could be preserved.

Chamberlain is a tragic figure in this story. Though he was sincere in his love of peace he was too shortsighted to realize that every concession made to Hitler only whetted the Führer appetite for more. Nor was he intelligent enough to see how the German dictator continually tricked him. Worst of all, Chamberlain did not understand that

by aiding Hitler in his bloodless conquests of new
territory, he was strengthening Germany and
weakening the position of the Western Allies, his
own country and France. In the end, his blunders
brought Great Britain to the brink of disaster.

By the middle of September, 1938, Chamberlain
had convinced the Czechoslovak government that
unless it peacefully ceded the Sudetenland to Hitler, the Führer would take it by force and destroy
Czechoslovakia. Meeting with the Nazi dictator on
September 22 at Godesburg, a picturesque little
town on the Rhine, Chamberlain informed Hitler
of his achievement. Czechoslovakia, he said, was
willing to hand over the Sudetenland to him. It
remained for them only to work out the details of
a peaceful turnover.

"I'm terribly sorry," the Führer replied. "But
your plan is no longer of any use."

Chamberlain sat up with a start. His owllike
face flushed with surprise and anger. The Nazi dictator, like a common blackmailer, was increasing
his demands. Hitler insisted that his new army
march into the Sudetenland at once. If the Czechs
resisted there would be war.

At a conference at Munich of the heads of government of Germany, Fascist Italy, France and
Great Britain on the night of September 29–30,

Hitler got his way. Chamberlain and Premier Daladier of France surrendered. They agreed that Hitler could march his troops into the Sudeten part of Czechoslovakia the next day.

I had watched Hitler at Godesburg. At that meeting he was in a highly nervous state. He seemed to be afraid that Chamberlain might call his bluff and that he would find himself in a war which, as the German generals later admitted, Germany would surely lose.

A week later at Munich Hitler was a changed man. In Munich he had first built up the Nazi party, staged his comic-opera Beer Hall Putsch and been sentenced to prison for treason. I shall never forget the light in his blazing eyes as he strutted down the steps of the *Führerhaus* after the midnight conference. He had not only made another bloodless conquest; he had humiliated the Czechs and the French and British as well. Yet he was not satisfied. Each new victory made him hungry for the next.

"That fellow Chamberlain," he remarked privately a few days later on his return to Berlin, "has spoiled my entry into Prague!"

He was determined to make that entry into the Czechoslovak capital at the head of his troops. And he soon made it—as the result of a piece of political trickery more brazen than even he had ever before attempted.

A few months passed. Shortly after midnight on March 15, 1939, the Führer of the German Reich received at his Chancellery in Berlin the President of what remained of Czechoslovakia. Not much remained. After gaining the Sudetenland Hitler had contrived by various threats and tricks to detach the Slovak part from Czechoslovakia. At the same time he unleashed a furious propaganda campaign based on the most outrageous lies. He claimed that what was left of the little Czech country was unmercifully persecuting the German minority in its midst. (We must remember that Hitler had always boasted that a big lie worked better than a small one.)

Dr. Emil Hácha, the Czech President, a senile old man with a weak heart, begged Hitler to be "generous" in allowing the Czechs "the right to live a national life." Whatever the Führer was, he was not generous. He turned on the aged Czech President with a torrent of abuse more violent even than that which he had inflicted on the Austrian Chancellor just a year before. We have the official secret German minutes of the meeting.

I have warned you [Hitler stormed] that unless Czechoslovakia mended its ways I would destroy this nation completely! It has not mended its ways! So I have given the order for the invasion by German troops and for the incorporation of Czechoslovakia into the German Reich!

President Hácha, one eyewitness later remembered, "sat as though turned to stone." His little nation was being swallowed by the German bully. But the German bully was not quite through with him. He must humble his guest with threats of Teutonic terror. Hitler informed Hácha that on that very morning the German army would enter "Czechia," as he now called it, from all sides. The Czechs, he said, had two choices. If they resisted, they would be "broken by brute force." If they surrendered he would be "generous," he said, and give the Czechs "a certain measure of national freedom."

And then came the cant and the threat of terror.

I am doing all this [Hitler continued] not from hatred but in order to protect Germany. If last autumn [at Munich] Czechoslovakia had not given in, the Czech people would have been exterminated! No one could have prevented me from doing it! The world would not have cared a jot.

I sympathize with the Czech people. That is why I have asked you to come here. This is the last good turn I can render the Czech people. Perhaps your visit may prevent the worst. The hours are passing. At 6:00 A.M. the troops will march in.

Hitler said that he wanted to give the Czech President a little time to think it over. "It is a grave decision, I realize," he concluded. "But I see dawning the possibility of a long period of peace between our two peoples. Should the decision be otherwise, I see the annihilation of Czechoslovakia."

With these words the Nazi tyrant dismissed his guest. It was now 2:15 in the morning of March 15, 1939. In and adjoining room Field Marshal Hermann Goering, Chief of the German Air Force, and Joachim von Ribbentrop, the arrogant Nazi Foreign Minister, continued Hitler's fiendish work. They hounded President Hácha to sign his country's death warrant. If he refused, Goering threatened, the German Air Force would destroy Prague that very morning, reducing it to a heap of rubble. They pushed a pen into the President's hand and bid him sign the surrender—or else.

At this point, according to a German witness who was standing just outside the room, Goering's voice was heard yelling for a doctor.

"Hácha has fainted!" the corpulent Field Marshal cried out.

For a moment the Nazi bullies feared that the prostrate Czech President might die on their hands. In that case, they would be accused of murdering him in the German Chancellery. Finally Hitler's personal physician, Dr. Theodor Morell, revived Hácha by means of injections. In this wretched state the President of Czechoslovakia signed the surrender to the ultimatum, which simply wiped out his country as an independent nation.

Still Hitler continued to lie. He issued an official communiqué, drawn up in advance of Hácha's arrival, saying that the Czech President had "confidently placed the fate of the Czech people and country in the hands of the Führer of the German Reich."

Hitler's deceit had reached a new high.

According to one of his secretaries, the Führer rushed from the signing into his office and exclaimed: "Children! This is the greatest day of my life! I shall go down in history as the greatest German!"

It did not occur to Adolf Hitler that the end of Czechoslovakia might be the beginning of the end for him. But, as we now know, it was. From this dawn of March 15, 1939—the ides of March—the road to war, to defeat, to disaster, stretched just ahead.

Once on that road and hurtling down it, Hitler, like Alexander and Napoleon before him, could not stop.

How Hitler Launched World War II

The next victim on Hitler's list after the German annexation of Czechoslovakia was Poland.

The Poles were a more difficult nut to crack. Their country was larger and more populous than Austria and Czechoslovakia. And they had potential allies who might come to their aid if attacked —France and Britain, and perhaps even Russia. These nations together could easily defeat Nazi Germany.

Of course it was impossible to be absolutely sure about an ally. France had been an ally of Czechoslokia's. But she had helped Britain betray that gallant little country to Hitler at Munich. France was also a formal ally of Poland. But in view of the past she was a doubtful one.

What about Great Britain, which had so lightly sacrificed the Czechs to Hitler? Prime Minister Chamberlain was finally beginning to understand the true intentions of the Führer. The Nazi dictator had opened Chamberlain's eyes when he swallowed up all of Czechoslovakia. Hitler was obviously a man no longer to be trusted. On March 31, just two weeks after the Führer entered Prague at the head of his army, Chamberlain informed Poland that if she were attacked Britain would come to her aid—along with France.

Hitler's reaction to Chamberlain's step was lightning quick—and typical. On April 4, 1939, he issued the Top Secret Directive for *Case White*. This was the code name for the plan to attack Poland. The dictator ordered the German army to be ready to carry it out on September 1.

In an attempt to discourage the British and French from coming to the aid of Poland, he next lined up Fascist Italy as an ally. The "Pact of Steel" was signed in Berlin on May 22. It obligated Italy to join Germany in case of war, no matter who started it.

The next day, on May 23, Hitler again called together his military chiefs in the Berlin Chancellery. This meeting is another milestone on the Nazi dictator's road to war. A secret record of it is among the captured documents. It gives us a revealing picture of the mind and character of Adolf Hitler at this stage of his strange career.

"There will be war! We must burn our boats!" he exclaimed to the German generals.

He had to attack in the East, he explained, in order to expand Germany's "living space" and procure more food for the Germans. He admitted that an attack might well bring "a showdown with the West"—that is, with England and France.

"England is our enemy!" he shouted, apparently forgetting how helpful Prime Minister Chamberlain had been when the Nazis occupied Austria and the Sudetenland. "The conflict with England," he added, "is a matter of life and death!"

Hitler was not quite sure what Soviet Russia would do. If the Russians allied themselves with the West, he said, "that would lead me to attack England and France with a few devastating blows."

Hitler then forecast how the war against England and France would be fought—a forecast that turned out to be surprisingly accurate. Belgium and Holland would be occupied first. Hitler wanted possession of little Belgium and Holland so as to give him a flanking position against France and also bases for naval and air warfare against the British Isles, which could then be blockaded.

His generals reminded their leader that these small countries were neutral.

"Declarations of neutrality can be ignored," Hitler retorted.

Germany's violation of Belgium's neutrality in 1914, at the outset of World War I, had outraged the civilized world. A second violation would outrage it even more. But Hitler did not care.

"Considerations of right and wrong," he snapped, "do not enter the matter! The aim must be to deal the enemy a smashing, decisive blow right at the start! We must force England to her knees!"

As for Poland, Hitler said, "she will be attacked at the first opportunity. We cannot expect a repetition of the Czech affair. There will be war!"

The question for the mad German dictator and his generals after this May meeting was: What kind of war? The generals tried to tell Hitler, as the fateful summer of 1939 began, that Germany simply did not possess the armed strength to take on Russia as well as Poland and the Western Powers. France and Britain were wooing the Soviet Union to come into an alliance against Hitler if he attacked Poland. If they succeeded—and

Russia did come in—the Führer, in the view of the generals, simply could not have his war. Or, if he did have it, he would surely lose it.

The dictator responded to this argument by making one of the shrewdest moves of his life. Despite his loathing of the Communists and indeed of the Communist Soviet Union, he decided to try to win over Russia to *his* side. It proved easier than anyone had suspected. But Hitler had to pay a stiff price.

The Soviet Union, like Nazi Germany, was ruled by an iron-willed dictator. His name was Josef Stalin, and for unscrupulousness, cruelty and double-dealing he was easily a match for Hitler. At the very moment Stalin was negotiating an alliance with the British and French military delegations that had come to Moscow, he began negotiating behind their backs a shabby deal with Adolf Hitler!

This cynical deal was signed in Moscow on the night of August 23, 1939, by Stalin and Ribbentrop, the German Foreign Minister. The Russians publicly agreed, in effect, to stay out of any war which Hitler might provoke. In return—though this part of the deal was kept secret—the two dictators agreed to divide up Poland. Further, Hitler acknowledged Russia's right to annex the Baltic states of Latvia and Estonia and Finland, which had belonged to her until 1919. These secret concessions were the price Hitler paid for keeping the Soviet Union out of the war.

Once again Hitler had outwitted his enemies. For this cold-blooded bargain with Stalin enabled Hitler to launch World War II when he did. Stalin thought he was saving Russia from a German attack, but this proved shortsighted. By one of those ironies of which history is so full, Stalin's act of unleashing German military power almost destroyed, as we shall shortly see, the Russian nation.

On August 22, when he knew that his deal with Stalin was certain, Hitler once more summoned his generals to hear his warlike thoughts. The meeting this time took place in the Führer's villa above Berchtesgaden in the Bavarian Alps. Several of the eminent army and navy participants in the secret conference took careful notes. These notes are among the captured German papers. They give us an intimate picture of the Nazi dictator on the eve of going to war. First, we can see his monumental egotism.

Essentially [Hitler said] all depends on me . . . because of my political talents. Probably no one will ever again have the confidence of the whole German people as I have. There will probably never again be a man with more authority.

He cited his deal with Stalin as an example of his political genius. He did not think the West would fight, though he gladly accepted the risk that it might. He did not want another Munich.

I am afraid [he said] that some dirty dog will make a proposal for mediation as at Munich.

This time, he went on, he wanted war. Working himself up to a state of hysterical fury, he admonished his generals:

Close your hearts to pity! Act brutally! The stronger man is right. Be harsh and remorseless! Be steeled against all signs of compassion! Whoever has pondered over this world order knows that its meaning lies in the success of the best by means of force.

That had long been his philosophy, as we have seen. He was now asking his generals to apply it in a practical manner. If the German military chiefs had any scruples about starting an unprovoked war, they did not mention them. But Hitler answered one question they might have raised.

I shall give a propaganda reason for starting the war. Never mind whether it is plausible or not. The victor will not be asked afterward whether he told the truth or not. In starting and waging a war it is not Right that matters, but Victory.

The next morning Hitler set "Y-Day" and "X-Hour" for the attack on Poland: August 26, 1939, at 4:30 A.M.

Twelve hours before "X-Hour" on the feverish evening of August 25, two events occurred which made Adolf Hitler shrink back from the abyss. One originated in London; the other in Rome.

The British Prime Minister had warned Hitler that his deal with Stalin would not prevent Britain from honoring its obligations to Poland. At 5:35 P.M. on August 25, Britain and Poland signed a formal Pact of Mutual Assistance. This meant that if Hitler assaulted Poland, he would have to fight Great Britain too. The Führer could no longer have any doubts of that.

A few minutes later Hitler received a second blow. His faithful friend and ally, Mussolini, informed him that if he attacked Poland, Italy would not join him in the war despite their treaty. Cursing his ally and the British, Hitler hastily postponed the attack.

"Führer considerably shaken!" General Franz Halder, the Chief of the Army General Staff, noted in his diary that evening after Hitler had drawn back from the precipice of war. But the next afternoon the General Staff Chief noted an abrupt change in the Leader.

"Führer very calm and clear," he jotted down in his journal at 3:22 P.M. There was reason for this, and the General's diary, which he kept meticulously hour by hour in shorthand, gives it. He had made up his mind to attack.

"Get everything ready! Attack starts September 1!" The order was telephoned by Hitler to the army high command.

There remained for the Führer only the little job of providing—as he had promised the generals he would do—a propaganda reason for starting the war. Hitler now pulled a typical piece of trickery. He gave orders to his secret police, the Gestapo, to carry out on the evening of August 31 a long-planned operation to fake a "Polish attack" on some German frontier stations. He could then launch his armies against Poland, claiming that he was merely repelling a Polish attack!

The plan was diabolical in concept. Some toughs belonging to the Nazi Elite Guard, the S.S., dressed in Polish army uniforms, were to carry out the

103

"Polish attack." And some poor prisoners from a concentration camp, a few of them dressed in Polish army uniforms, were to be brought to the scene and left dead to give a touch of reality to the "Polish attack."

But even before this treachery was perpetrated, Hitler took the final decision that made World War II inevitable. At thirty minutes past noon on the last day of August, 1939, while the British government was still trying to make him see reason, the German warlord, as he now saw himself, took the last fatal step to war. He scrawled his signature on the following order:

SUPREME COMMANDER OF THE ARMED FORCES
MOST SECRET

Berlin, August 31, 1939

Now that all the *political possibilities* of disposing by peaceful means of a situation on the Eastern frontier which is intolerable for Germany *are exhausted,* I have determined on a solution by force.

The *attack on Poland* is to be carried out in accordance with the preparations for *Case White.**

Date of attack: September 1, 1939

Time of attack: 4:45 A.M.

(signed) Adolf Hitler

* The italics are Hitler's.

As the last day of peace ticked on, Adolf Hitler

was in fine fettle. At 6:00 P.M. General Halder noted in his diary: "Führer calm; has slept well."

When darkness settled over Europe on that evening of August 31, 1939, a million and a half German troops moved up to their final position on the Polish border for the jump-off at dawn. At half a dozen frontier stations the Gestapo carried out its faked "Polish attacks," leaving a few concentration camp prisoners lying dead.

Berlin itself was quiet. The German people, though worked up by Nazi propaganda about the seriousness of the Polish situation, did not expect war.

I finished my last broadcast from Berlin to America shortly before four o'clock in the morning. It was already the first day of September, and close to Hitler's "X-Hour," though I did not know it. The night began to fade as I drove back from the Broadcasting House to the Adlon Hotel. There was no traffic. The houses were dark. The people were asleep and perhaps—for all I knew—had gone to bed hoping for the best, for peace.

Forty-five minutes later, as day broke on September 1, 1939, Hitler's armies poured across the Polish frontier. Overhead great clouds of German bombers quickly penetrated Poland and let loose their destruction from the skies. In the Atlantic waters around the British Isles German submarines waited, submerged, to see whether Great Britain—along with France—would honor its word to Poland and come into the war against Germany.

On Sunday, September 3, after some hesitation, the governments of Britain and France gave a determined answer to that crucial question. On the previous day they had warned Hitler that unless he stopped fighting and withdrew his armies from Poland they would declare war against Germany. When he did not do so they declared war.

That Sunday in Berlin was a beautiful, sunny, end-of-the-summer day. At precisely 9:00 A.M. the British Ambassador, Sir Nevile Henderson arrived at the German Foreign Office to present an ultimatum: Unless Hitler informed him by 11:00 A.M. that he was pulling his troops out of Poland, there would be war between Britain and Germany.

Dr. Paul Schmidt, the German official who received the Ambassador, hurried down the Wilhelmstrasse to present the ultimatum to Hitler. When he had finished translating it to the Führer, he says:

There was complete silence. Hitler sat immobile, gazing before him. After a long interval he turned to Ribbentrop [his foreign minister].

"What now?" Hitler asked.

France declared war a few hours later that Sunday. At nine o'clock in the evening Hitler departed for the front to command his armies personally. Before leaving he did two things.

He got off a long letter to Mussolini, the ally who had abandoned him at the last moment. "I am aware," he wrote, "that the struggle is for life and death." He was disappointed that Italy had not honored her word by coming into the war. But he kept his feelings to himself. A friendly Italy, even though not in the war, could still be helpful to him. But even more helpful could be the new friend, Russia.

At 6:50 that Sunday evening Hitler dispatched a message to Stalin inviting the Soviet Union to join in the attack on Poland. They had secretly agreed, it will be remembered, to divide up Poland. If they shared the booty, why should they not share the blame? A Russian aggression against Poland would take some of the blame off Hitler. Stalin, as we shall see, did not need much urging.

The fateful Sunday of September 3, 1939, was

now passing into history. But in the gathering darkness one more event occurred which remains to be chronicled.

At exactly 9:00 P.M., at the moment Hitler's train was pulling out of the darkened railroad station in Berlin for the Polish front, the German navy, which had little to do in Poland, struck in the West.

Without warning, the submarine U-30 torpedoed and sank the British liner *Athenia* 200 miles west of the British Isles. Of the 1,400 passengers, 112, of whom 28 were Americans, were drowned.*

World War II, provoked cold-bloodedly by Adolf Hitler, had begun.

---

* Throughout the war the German government solemnly denied that one of its submarines had sunk the *Athenia*. It publicly charged that Winston Churchill, then First Lord of the British Admiralty, had arranged to have it sunk in order to help bring America into the war. Only at the postwar trials of the German war criminals at Nuremberg did the truth emerge. Grand Admiral Karl Doenitz, one of the defendants at the trial, admitted that the U-30 had sunk the *Athenia*. In 1939 he had been commander of submarines.

Hitler's Astounding Early Victories

Adolf Hitler's victories during the first three years of World War II were stupendous. They exceeded his wildest dreams.

His armies, to begin with, overran Poland in three weeks. The French and British forces might have taken some of the pressure off the Poles by attacking in the West. There the Germans had only a few weak, defensive divisions. But the Western Allies remained idle.

No wonder that the conflict in the West soon became known as the "phony war" or, as the Germans called it, the *Sitzkrieg*—"the sit-down war." Along the Franco-German border the rival armies sat behind their fortifications and declined to fight. It was uncanny.

One autumn day in 1939 I visited the so-called "Western front" along the Rhine. From the German side of the river I could see the French troops on the far bank working on their fortifications. One group of them was playing an impromptu soccer-football game. Neither side fired on the other. A strange kind of war!

Poland, where I had followed the German army for a few days, was different. The cities and towns were in shambles from bombing and artillery fire. Everywhere was the stench of the unburied dead.

It was in Poland that the figure of Adolf Hitler as the mighty German warlord quickly emerged. I saw him at Danzig on September 19, 1939, and noted in my dairy that he had never before looked so imperious. He strutted about as if he were Caesar and Napoleon combined.

I noted, too, his fury. He was in a terrible rage one afternoon because Warsaw, the Polish capital, still refused to surrender, though most of the rest of Poland had been conquered—with the help of Russia's Red army!* He had had to wait outside

---

* At dawn on September 17, Soviet troops had attacked Poland from the east in flagrant violation of the Soviet Union's nonaggression treaty with Poland. This was one of the most treacherous acts of the war. Hitler and Stalin promptly divided up Poland between them.

the burning city for three days. This had forced
him to postpone his triumphal entry into the
vanquished city. It made him raving mad.

These spasms of violent rage were to grow in
frequency and intensity as the war continued. We
shall see them contributing to the disintegration
of the Nazi conqueror. But in the first war years,
when all went well, Hitler usually managed to
keep them under control. Yet his megalomania,†
the fatal disease of all dictators and world conquerors, could not be kept in check.

We can glimpse Hitler in the grip of this disease
as he again addressed his generals on November
23, 1939. I found the secret records of the talk
in the captured files of the German Army High
Command.

Six weeks before, shortly after the conquest of
Poland, Hitler had issued a directive for the
attack against the Anglo-French armies in the
West. The big offensive was to begin with a surprise onslaught through the neutral countries of
Belgium and Holland so as to outflank the British
and French forces.

The German generals had balked at attacking

† Megalomania is a mental disease marked by delusions of
grandeur in the patient.

in the West on the ground that the army was not yet ready. A few of them had even objected to violating the neutrality of the two small countries. The Nazi warlord called them in to put some iron in their veins.

My decision [Hitler thundered] is unchangeable! I shall attack France and England at the most favorable and earliest moment. Breach of the neutrality of Belgium and Holland is of no importance. No one will question that when we have won. We shall not justify the breach of neutrality as idiotically as in 1914.

Hitler seemed piqued at his generals for their slowness in recognizing his genius.

As the last factor in this struggle [he said] I must—in all modesty—name my own person.

Irreplaceable!

Neither a military man nor a civilian could replace me! I am convinced of the powers of my intellect. No one has ever achieved what I have achieved! I have led the German people to a great height—even if the world does hate us now.

The fate of the Reich depends only on me! I shall act accordingly! I shall shrink from nothing. I shall annihilate everyone who is opposed to me!

No German general who listened to Hitler that November day in the first year of the war—and all the leading generals were present—could have had any further doubts about his Commander in Chief. The tyrant who now held their fate in his hands—and the fate of Germany and, as it then seemed, of the world—had become beyond any question a dangerous, irresponsible megalomaniac.

Yet in the next seven months Hitler could be so cool and cunning in his calculations and so bold in carrying them out that few could doubt that he well might be the military genius he claimed to be.

Over the objections of most of his generals, he planned and carried out the daring operation by which Denmark and Norway were militarily occupied in April, 1940. At dawn on April 9, German freight boats, accompanied by naval ships, simply sneaked into the five main Norwegian ports as well as into the port of Copenhagen, the capital of Denmark. German troops sprang out of the ships' holds and occupied the towns with scarcely a shot.

In fact, Denmark capitulated within two hours. The plucky Norwegians, helped by the Allies and their own mountainous terrain, held out longer—until June.

By the end of that month Hitler's armies had overrun the continent of Western Europe. On

May 10, 1940, they struck across the borders of Holland and Belgium and drove quickly into France. Within six weeks the campaign was over. The low countries had surrendered as had France —France which had held out successfully for four years in World War I. And the British Expeditionary Corps had been driven across the channel to England.

Once again the Nazi conqueror had shown his daring. Against the advice of many of his top generals, he had decided to strike through the hilly, heavily wooded Ardennes Forest in Belgium with his great tank armies. The French and British thought an armored attack here was impossible. But it wasn't.

Within ten days German tanks reached the English Channel at Abbeville, cutting off the British armies and the flower of the French forces. "The Führer is beside himself with joy!" General Jodl, one of his chief aides, scribbled in his dairy the night the news from Abbeville was received.

France formally surrendered unconditionally on June 22, 1940, at Compiègne. This was the very spot where the Germans had given up and signed the Armistice at the end of World War I. In order to sweeten his revenge, Hitler had insisted on the French surrendering there.

I was at Compiègne and had the chance to observe Adolf Hitler at the moment of his greatest conquest. It was the high point of his astonishing life.

The surrender ceremony took place on one of the loveliest June days I have ever seen in France. A warm sun beat down upon the little clearing in the woods as Hitler stepped up jauntily onto the granite block of the Allied War Memorial to read the words of the inscription:

HERE ON THE ELEVENTH OF NOVEMBER, 1918, SUCCUMBED THE CRIMINAL PRIDE OF THE GERMAN EMPIRE—VANQUISHED BY THE FREE PEOPLES WHICH IT TRIED TO ENSLAVE.

Standing there in the bright June sun and the silence, Hitler read the scarring words. I looked for the expression on his face when he had finished. I had seen that face often at the great moments of his life. Now it lit up first with hatred as he pondered the words. Then it changed to contempt and ended in triumph.

The German warlord could now take his revenge. He strode over to the old armistice sleeping car, which German army engineers had removed from the nearby museum to the exact spot where it had stood in 1918. Hitler took the very seat occupied by Marshal Foch when the Allied generalissimo had sat in the car and dictated the armistice terms to the Germans at the end of the previous war. He listened while General Wilhelm Keitel, Chief of the Supreme Command, read *his* terms to the French. Then he departed for Paris.

In the beautiful capital of France on the banks of the Seine, Hitler experienced one intense emotion. He visited the tomb of the great French conqueror, Napoleon Bonaparte. For nearly an hour he gazed contemplatively at it.

"That," he remarked to his aides afterward, "was the greatest and finest moment of my life!" It was obvious that he now considered himself the twentieth century's Napoleon. How he relished the role!

Adolf Hitler had seemingly reached the pinnacle. He had conquered most of Europe—from the Vistula River to the Atlantic Ocean, from the North Cape high above the Arctic Circle in Norway to the Pyrenees Mountains on the border of Spain. Only Britain held out against him. With her armies driven from the mainland and her island virtually defenseless, Hitler was sure the

British would give up too. If not, he could easily conquer them.

But now a curious and fateful thing happened. The Nazi conqueror did not know what to do with his greatest of victories. He had no idea what move to make next. He hesitated, and this was fatal.

It is easy to see now why he faltered at the moment of dizzy success. Hitler's mind, like the minds of his generals, was landlocked. Its horizons were limited to land warfare against neighboring nations. It was ignorant of the oceans. In fact Hitler had a horror of the sea.

"On land I am a hero," he told one of his field marshals, "but on water I am a coward."

To be sure, only a few miles of water stood between Hitler's victorious armies on the Normandy coast and the defenseless British beaches across the narrow English Channel. But the Nazi warlord had made no preparations—or even plans —to ferry his troops across it.

This might have been difficult in view of British naval power. But the Norwegian campaign had shown that the German air force could neutralize the British navy along the sea coast. Even if a few German regiments had got across the Channel at the end of June they might have conquered

Britain. For the British Expeditionary Force had lost most of its weapons in France. For the moment there was no armed British land force of any consequence to oppose the invasion.

By August the British had had time to reorganize their army and to find arms—some of them hurriedly brought over from America. In order to defeat them Hitler would now have to land a large force on the English beaches.

Late in August he issued his invasion orders. But it was now too late. The German navy was incapable of conveying across the Channel enough troops to assure success. The famed R.A.F.—the Royal Air Force—was proving itself a match for the Luftwaffe, the German air force, in defending the skies over Britain.

The invasion of Britain was never attempted. Nor could Hitler be persuaded to help the Italians, who had finally come into the war on his side after France's fall. Italy needed German aid to enable her to drive the hard-pressed British out of the Mediterranean and Egypt. This could easily have been accomplished at this time had the Germans and the Italians acted together. They might have finished Britain by severing one of her main lifelines. But Hitler did not understand naval warfare nor comprehend overseas operations.

He decided instead to continue his land warfare against another neighbor. He decided to turn on his friend and ally, the Soviet Union. This was a grave mistake. It led to his doom.

Why did Hitler, who had conquered most of the European continent so easily and so quickly, take this fatal decision? No other conqueror from the West had ever succeeded in taking Russia. Not Charles XII of Sweden. Not Hitler's idol, Napoleon.

The answer is that Hitler had begun to believe in his own legend as the invincible conqueror. In February, 1941, as preparations for the surprise attack on Russia proceeded, he exclaimed to his generals: "When *Barbarossa* (the code word for the Russian campaign) commences, the world will hold its breath!" He fooled himself into believing that Russia, as he had written in *Mein Kampf*, could be had for the taking.

There was also a practical reason for Hitler's decision. This sprang from his overpowering greed. He intended to destroy Russia as a nation and rule it for the benefit of the German "Master

Race." It would supply food and minerals and cheap slave labor for Germany.

Hitler's increasing lust for cruelty also was a factor. He ordered that Russia's two great cities, Moscow and Leningrad, be "wiped off the face of the earth"—along with their millions of inhabitants. He deliberately intended to starve millions of other Russians to death.

There is no doubt [says one of his decrees] that as a result of our plan many millions of persons in Russia will be starved to death.

As the first winter of the Russian campaign approached, Reich Marshal Goering (as he now was titled) told Count Ciano, the Italian Foreign Minister:

This year between twenty and thirty million persons will die of hunger in Russia. In the camps for Russian prisoners they have begun to eat each other. Perhaps it is well that it is so, for certain nations must be decimated.

Hitler's first victories in Russia, after the surprise attack began on June 22, 1941, were staggering. As autumn came his armies, after advancing hundreds of miles, were approaching Moscow and Leningrad. The fertile grain fields of the Ukraine were being quickly overrun. As a matter of fact, not only Hitler but even the military authorities in the West—in London and Washington—believed that the Soviet Union was finished.

On October 3, 1941, Hitler rushed back from the Eastern front to Berlin to announce that to the world. In a broadcast speech heard around the globe he said:

I declare today—without any reservation—that the enemy in the East has been struck down and will never rise again.

The Russians were certainly down, but not out. And now two factors came to their aid: the winter's cold and snow, which had defeated Napoleon's *Grande Armée* in Russia; and Hitler's faulty generalship.

With the cruel Russian winter approaching, the generals wanted to strike for Moscow and capture the capital. But Hitler decided he wanted first to take Leningrad in the north and finish the occupation of the Ukraine grain belt in the south. By the time he had regrouped his armies for the onslaught on Moscow it was too late. Winter and heavy snows had arrived. And the Red army had had time to recover from its early setbacks.

The week between December 6 and 11, 1941, was a crucial one in the life and career of Adolf Hitler.

On December 5, his armies arrived at the gates of Moscow. The next day, during a blizzard, they were thrown back. It was the first German defeat of the war. And for the first time Hitler's armies were forced to retreat. It was a blow from which he and his troops never recovered.

Hitler now compounded his faulty generalship with a political blunder. On December 7 the Japanese had treacherously bombed Pearl Harbor. This had brought the United States into the war —against Japan, but not against Germany. Hitler had made vague promises to join the Japanese in a war against America. He now honored them. On December 11, 1941, he declared war on the United States.

The year 1941, then, marks a fateful turning point in the life of Hitler the Conqueror. He deliberately—out of his own madness—added to his enemies the two potentially strongest military powers in the world: Russia and the United States. In the long run Germany could not be a match for them and for Britain as well.

That would be proved the next year, in 1942, which would bring the final great turning point. From then on, the road for Adolf Hitler stretched down to utter disaster.

The Great Turning Point

The strain of war began to tell on Adolf Hitler. He insisted on personally directing every detail of the operations of a huge army on the 1,500-mile Russian front. This was too much for any man to attempt to do.

Also, he could not stand defeats. In the drifting snows and subzero temperatures of Russia during that winter of 1941–42, the German armies nearly perished. Napoleon had suffered a similar disaster in an equally cruel Russian winter during another famous retreat from Moscow. And that had quickly led to his end.

When Count Ciano saw the Führer early in the spring of 1942 he found him looking weary and worn.

"The winter months in Russia have borne heavily upon him," the Italian Foreign Minister noted in his diary, and added: "I see for the first time that he has many gray hairs."

Dr. Joseph Goebbels, the Nazi Propaganda Minister and one of Hitler's closest confidants, expressed shock in his diary at his master's appearance.

I noted that he has become quite gray. He told me that he had to fight off attacks of giddiness. He truly worries me.

Goebbels noted another thing about the Führer.

He has a physical revulsion against frost and snow. What torments him most is that the country [Russia] is still covered with snow.

As a result of the Führer's folly in refusing to allow his troops to retreat in that snow, many German formations were surrounded by the Russians and captured. On the other hand, there is little doubt that Hitler's fierce determination to hold on saved the German armies, for the time being, from catastrophe.

This led him into the error, however, of convincing himself that he alone could hold his armies together and ultimately lead them to victory. All that first winter of the Russian campaign, as disasters mounted, Hitler fired field marshals and generals one after the other. He himself took over as Commander in Chief of the Army.

He was now not only Supreme Warlord, Supreme Commander of the Armed Forces (which included the air force and navy) but actual commander of the army. As such he resumed the offensive in Russia as soon as summer came in 1942.

At first, as usual, Hitler's fortunes prospered—on all fronts. By the end of June his brilliant commander in North Africa, General Erwin Rommel, had driven the British back into Egypt. (The Germans were now fighting alongside the Italians in Africa.) Rommel's Italian-German armies had reached El Alamein. This was only sixty-five miles from Alexandria and the delta of the Nile. Britain's position in the Mediterranean, in Egypt, in the Middle East, seemed doomed. Prime Minister Churchill, who had replaced Chamberlain in 1940, later admitted that for him this was one of the darkest periods of the war.

But the apparent debacle in Egypt was not the only cause of Churchill's gloom. In the Atlantic

Hitler's submarines were sinking an average of 700,000 tons of Anglo-American shipping a month. This was more than could be replaced in the shipyards of Britain and the United States. And the loss of so many precious cargoes deprived the British of desperately needed food and arms which were being shipped to them from the Americas. If the sinkings continued at such a rate Great Britain would be starved out of the war.

But it was in Russia that summer that Hitler's hopes rose highest. The new offensive was launched on June 22, the anniversary of Germany's sneak attack on the Soviet Union. By August 23, units of the German Sixth Army reached the Volga River just north of Stalingrad. They cut off the last route by which the oil of the Caucasus could reach the main Russian armies and industries to the north. Without oil, a modern army cannot fight. The Russians, like the British, faced disaster.

The sources of Russia's oil were also on the verge of being captured by the Germans. By August 25, Nazi tanks had reached a point in the Caucasus only fifty miles from the principal Soviet oil fields at Grozny. Once again, as in the previous December when his troops got to the suburbs of Moscow, Hitler seemed to be on the point of knocking the Soviet Union out of the war.

He told his generals that the Russians "were finished." He had told the world the same thing the previous autumn. And then he committed a serious strategic blunder. Now, at the summer's end in 1942, in the same belief that the Russians "were finished," he repeated the blunder.

Even an amateur strategist could see that the German armies on the Volga and deep in the Caucasus were overextended. They were vulnerable on their long flanks to Russian counterattacks which, if successful, would cut them off.

General Halder, the Chief of the General Staff, pointed out to Hitler that Stalin had amassed a million and a half fresh troops for these counterattacks. When Halder urged that the German armies be pulled back, the warlord flew into a rage. He dismissed Halder and appointed a new General Staff Chief named Kurt Zeitzler.

Zeitzler gave Hitler the same advice. This sent the Führer into a fresh tantrum.

"Where the German soldier sets foot," he shouted at Zeitzler, "there he remains!" The warlord thereupon forebade any withdrawal from Stalingrad or from the Caucasus.

From this foolish command, and from a similar one given by Hitler to Rommel in North Africa, there followed terrible disaster for the Germans.

In Egypt the British, aided by American supplies of tanks, guns and planes, had rallied. Under a new and resourceful commander, General Bernard Montgomery, the British Eighth Army attacked Rommel's Italo-German desert forces at El Alamein on the night of October 23, 1942. By November 2 Montgomery's tanks and troops had scored a devastating breakthrough. Rommel's forces were threatened with total destruction unless they immediately pulled back.

Rommel wired Hitler at his headquarters two thousand miles away for permission to withdraw some forty miles. The warlord's response was found in Rommel's papers after the General's suicide.

. . . There can be no other consideration save that of holding fast, of not retreating one step, of throwing every gun and every man into the battle. You can show your troops no other way than that which leads to victory or to death.

Adolf Hitler

Reluctantly and against his better judgment, Rommel obeyed. On November 4, when he had lost more than half his force of ninety-six thousand men, he risked Hitler's wrath and decided to save what was left of his armies. In fifteen days he retreated not forty miles but seven hundred miles! The Führer never forgave him.

The Battle of El Alamein was the beginning of the end for Adolf Hitler. It was followed by the greatest disaster ever suffered by German arms— a disaster which could have been avoided had the Nazi warlord not lost all contact with reality. His mind was already disintegrating, though his fierce will power remained as strong as ever. This combination led to catastrophe.

The Russian counterattack on the Don front *behind* Stalingrad, of which the German generals had warned Hitler, was launched in a blizzard at dawn on November 19, 1942. Within twenty-four hours the Russians had broken clear through the German positions and threatened to cut off the Sixth Army in Stalingrad.

General Zeitzler urged a hasty retreat from that battered city, where German and Soviet troops were locked in savage street-to-street fighting. The mere suggestion threw the Nazi warlord into another fit.

"I won't leave the Volga!" he yelled at his General Staff Chief. He issued strict orders that the Sixth Army must stand fast in Stalingrad.

It did. And on November 22, only four days

after the beginning of the Soviet counteroffensive, the German Sixth Army found itself cut off. Two Russian armies met at Kalash, forty miles *behind* Stalingrad on the Don bend.

In vain General Friedrich Paulus, Commander of the Sixth Army, radioed Hitler for permission to fight his way out. The Führer refused. He promised relief, which started but never arrived.

Three days before Christmas General Zeitzler had a showdown meeting with his warlord.

I begged Hitler [he later reported] to authorize the breakout. I pointed out this was absolutely the last chance to save Paulus' army. Hitler would not give way. In vain I described to him the conditions in Stalingrad: the despair of the starving soldiers . . . the wounded expiring for lack of proper attention, while thousands froze to death.

Hitler, says Zeitzler, remained deaf to all his pleas. He also remained deaf to the more pitiful pleas of Paulus. On January 24, 1943, the Sixth Army Commander radioed Hitler asking that he be permitted to surrender. The Russians, he explained, had reduced the Sixth Army to two separated fragments holding out in the snow-covered rubble of Stalingrad. And he added:

Troops without ammunition or food . . . Effective command no longer possible. 18,000 wounded without any supplies or dressings or drugs . . . Further defense senseless. Collapse inevitable. Sixth Army requests immediate permission to surrender in order to save the lives of the remaining troops.

Hitler's reply was found in the captured Nazi papers.

Surrender is forbidden! Sixth Army will hold their positions to the last man and the last round.

Such was the mad warlord's hold on his generals that Paulus obeyed—or tried to. But the agony of the Sixth Army could not be prolonged much longer. On January 30, the tenth anniversary of Hitler's becoming chancellor, General Paulus radioed the Führer: "Final collapse cannot be delayed more than twenty-four hours."

The Supreme Commander's reactions to this message was to promote—by radio—General Paulus to field marshal! There was a sordid reason for this and Hitler gave it. "There is no record in military history," he told his staff, "of a German field marshal being taken prisoner."

Field Marshal Paulus spoiled the record. The next day he simply gave up, along with twenty-four other generals and ninety-one thousand German soldiers.

In his well-heated headquarters far away in East Prussia Hitler raged and ranted. A stenographic account of part of his ravings survives among the captured documents. It gives a revealing picture of the Nazi conqueror at this great turning point in his life.

The scene is the map room at headquarters on February 1, 1943. Hitler is surrounded by his generals—Zeitzler, Keitel, Jodl and others. As usual he does most of the talking.

Paulus should have shot himself, just as the old commanders who threw themselves on their swords when they saw that the cause was lost. Even Varus gave his slave the order: "Now kill me!"

Then Hitler philosophized on life and death.

What is life? Life is the nation. The individual must die anyway. Beyond the life of the individual is the nation.

How can anyone be afraid of the moment of death, with which he can free himself from this misery? If his duty doesn't chain him to this vale of tears? Na!

So many people have to die. And then a man like Paulus besmirches the heroism of so many others at the last minute. He could have freed himself from all sorrow and ascended into eternity and national immortality. But he prefers to go to Moscow!

... That's the last Field Marshal I shall appoint in this war!

There was not a word of sympathy or grief from Hitler, sitting in his comfortable headquarters far behind the front, for the more than one hundred thousand German soldiers who had been slaughtered in the carnage of Stalingrad. Not a word about the sufferings of the ninety-one thousand German soldiers who survived. At that very moment these men, half-starved, frostbitten, many of them wounded, were hobbling over the ice and snow. They clutched their blood-caked blankets over their heads against the cold that was twenty-four degrees below zero as they wearily trudged along toward the dreary, frozen prisoner-of-war camps in Siberia.

Nor was there a single word from Hitler about his own responsibility for the greatest military defeat in German history.

The disintegration of the man was accelerating, both in mind and body. He began to take increasing amounts of drugs to relieve his nervous tensions. The effects of these were plainly visible.

General Heinz Guderian saw Hitler shortly

after the Stalingrad debacle. It had been fourteen months since the General had last seen the war-lord and he hardly recognized him.

Hitler's hands trembled [Guderian recalled later]. He stooped. He stared fixedly. His eyes had a tendency to bulge and were dull and lusterless. There were red spots on his cheeks. He was more excitable than ever. When angered he lost all self-control.

This was a man now doomed—and by his own folly. He had deliberately provoked against him a coalition of military powers which was much too strong for Germany to resist. The first consequences had just been seen on the burning sands of El Alamein and in the snows of Stalingrad.

Already the Americans, who Hitler had once said could never land in Europe, had landed in North Africa. With their British allies they were closing in on the German-Italian forces in Tunisia. There, when the spring of 1943 came, more Germans would surrender than had at Stalingrad.

Hitler's fate was sealed, though he managed to hold it off for two more bloody years.

PART 4

THE FALL OF ADOLF HITLER

Hitler's "New Order"

One of Adolf Hitler's cruelest dreams was shattered at El Alamein and Stalingrad. This was his plan for establishing a so-called New Order.

Hitler's grotesque and gruesome New Order was a throwback to an ancient Teutonic barbarism. What the mad dictator planned was a Nazi-ruled Europe whose resources would be exploited for the profit of Germany. The captive peoples would be made the slaves of the German Master Race. And what Hitler called the "undesirable elements"—above all, the Jews, but also many Slavs in the East—would be exterminated.

The conquered Slavic peoples were the Czechs, Poles and Russians. Hitler laid down the general line for their treatment in 1942. "The Slavs," he ordered, "are to work for us. Insofar as we don't need them they may die. . . . We are the masters. We come first."

The Communist political leaders in Russia and the upper classes and intellectuals in Poland were to be literally exterminated. Thus in regard to the Poles a captured memorandum signed by Hitler states:

. . . The Polish gentry must cease to exist! However cruel this may sound, they must be exterminated.
. . . Also all representatives of the Polish intelligentsia [intellectuals] are to be exterminated. This sounds cruel, but such is the law of life.

The "law of life," as Hitler's diseased mind and soul understood it, was applied to most of captive Europe. The ensuing bloody nightmare has no parallel in that ancient continent's experience.

Seven and a half million foreign civilians—men, women and children—were forced to work as slave labor in Germany. Many of them were beaten, half starved, housed in hovels not fit for cattle, and forced to work from dawn to dark. Millions more were placed in concentration camps, where most of them died or were put to death.

But the worst fate was reserved by the Führer

for the Jews. He was determined, he said, to make Europe "Jew-free."

He almost succeeded. Of Europe's ten million Jews, nearly five million were massacred in Hitler's gas chambers—and their bodies burned in his specially constructed furnaces. Another three-quarters of a million Jews were slain by the machine guns of the so-called *Einsatzgruppen*—Special Task Forces. This was the choice Nazi S.S. group which specialized in slaughtering Jews in Poland and in Russia by gunfire.

I remember one of the judges at the Nuremberg Trials interrupting Otto Ohlendorf, who led one of the special S.S. groups in Russia. Ohlendorf, like so many S.S. thugs, was a university-trained intellectual. Before the war he had been a professor in a German university. He was testifying about the ninety thousand men, women and children his detachment had massacred in Russia.

"For what reason were the children massacred?" the judge asked.

OHLENDORF: The order was that the Jewish population should be totally exterminated.

THE JUDGE: Including the children?

OHLENDORF: Yes.

THE JUDGE: Were all the Jewish children murdered?

OHLENDORF: Yes.

The slaughter of more than five million human beings who happened to be Jews was the macabre consequence and the shattering cost of the anti-Semitic madness which came over Adolf Hitler in his youthful days as a tramp in Vienna. It was a disease he imparted to—or shared with—many of his German followers.

There were many other cruel aspects of the New Order. They included the kidnaping of children in the conquered lands for work in Germany; inhuman "medical experiments" on thousands of Jews and captive persons, who died as the result; the summary execution of many thousands of "hostages" in the occupied lands—a barbarous practice which civilized countries had long abandoned; and plans to "wipe off the face of the earth," as Hitler put it, Russia's two greatest cities, Moscow and Leningrad, along with their millions of inhabitants.

Though Hitler failed to capture the two great Russian cities, he did demonstrate how a town which he *had* captured could be wiped off the face of the earth. This is what happened to Lidice in Czechoslovakia on June 10, 1942.

The warlord was in a fury because two Czech patriots had assassinated Reinhard Heydrich, the so-called Nazi "Protector" of the former Czech nation. Heydrich was also the number two man in the Nazi Gestapo—the secret police. A thug of diabolical cast, he was one of the most hated Nazis in the occupied lands.

Hitler took savage revenge for his assassination. According to captured Gestapo records, 1,131 Czechs, including 201 women, were immediately executed as a reprisal. But of all of Hitler's "reprisals," what was done to the peaceful little village of Lidice will perhaps be longest remembered by the civilized world.

On the morning of June 9, German security police arrived at Lidice and surrounded the village. No one was allowed to leave. One boy of twelve, taking fright, tried to steal away. He was shot down and killed. All the men in the village were locked up in barns.

The next day the German police shot them all— a total of 172 men and boys over sixteen. Seven women were taken to nearby Prague and executed. The remaining women, mostly wives of slain Czechs, were sent to a concentration camp in Germany.

What of the children under sixteen? There were ninety of these. They were all carted off to another concentration camp and later sent to German orphanages and homes where they were given new German names. They were to be brought up as Germans.

"Every trace of them has been lost," the Czechoslovakian government reported after the war. Later, seventeen of them were traced to Bavaria and in 1947 sent home.

But there was no home in Lidice. Hitler had wiped it off the face of the earth. As soon as the men had been massacred and the wives and children carted off to a concentration camp, the German security police burned down the village, dynamited the ruins and leveled them off with bulldozers.

The site remains in that condition today—a weird monument to Hitler's New Order.

Fortunately for mankind the New Order was destroyed in its infancy—but not until the captive peoples of Europe had lived through the nightmare of its first horrors. The New Order was not brought down by any revolt of the German people against such barbarism but by the defeat of German arms, the consequent overrunning of Germany by the victorious Allies, and the fall of Adolf Hitler.

The Plot to Kill Hitler

Shortly after dawn on the warm, sunny morning of July 20, 1944, Colonel Count Klaus Schenk von Stauffenberg, Chief of Staff of the Replacement Army, drove out past the bombed-out buildings of Berlin to the airport at Rangsdorf.

In his bulging brief case were papers concerning new divisions for Hitler's crumbling armies. He had been commanded to report on them to the Führer at 1:00 P.M. at Supreme Headquarters in East Prussia.

In between the papers, wrapped in a shirt, was a time bomb. Stauffenberg was confident that it would blast Adolf Hitler to pieces.

In Berlin a small number of army officers stood by. As soon as the Nazi warlord was dead, they intended to seize the capital, declare the Nazi regime overthrown and sue for peace.

Chief among these officers were Field Marshal Erwin von Witzleben, one of Hitler's top field commanders, and General Ludwig Beck, a former chief of the General Staff. The generals and their accomplices knew that the war was lost. By eliminating Hitler in one bold stroke they hoped to get a peace that would leave the German nation with some chance for survival.

For more than a year following the German disasters at Stalingrad and in North Africa the war had gone from bad to worse for the Nazi dictator. His stupendous conquests of the first war years were being rapidly lost.

By the summer of 1944 half of Italy was gone, and most of Russia. Six weeks before Colonel Stauffenberg set out on his fateful errand to assassinate Hitler, General Dwight D. Eisenhower's Anglo-American armies had landed on the beaches of Normandy. They were now threatening to break out toward Paris and drive the Germans out of France.

Berlin itself, like most of the other great cities of Germany, was in shambles from the Anglo-American bombing. The United States Air Force bombed by day and the Royal Air Force by night, allowing no respite to the dazed and weary inhabitants trudging about the smoking ruins. The Germans were being repaid a hundred times for the bombings they had initiated: of Warsaw and Rotterdam and London and Coventry.

The once vaunted German-Italian Axis, which had struck such terror throughout Europe, lay in ruins. Benito Mussolini, Hitler's Italian partner in crime, had been overthrown. Summoned by the King of Italy to the royal palace in Rome on the evening of July 25, 1943, the Italian dictator had been arrested and taken off to the police station in an ambulance.

Adolf Hitler could scarcely help seeing the handwriting on the wall. After Mussolini's fall would it not be his turn next? Not, he concluded, if he could help it. He acted—for one of the last times of the war—with ice-cold determination to restore his position and that of Mussolini. He ordered German troops in Italy to take over.

Drive into Rome [he commanded] and arrest the whole Italian government! Get the King and the whole bunch right away! Arrest the Crown Prince and the whole gang! Pack them into a plane and off with them!

Some of the generals asked what was to be

done with the Vatican, the world center of the Roman Catholic Church, which was situated in the heart of Rome.

I'll go right into the Vatican [Hitler answered]. Do you think the Vatican embarrasses me? We'll take that over right away. The entire diplomatic corps are in there. That rabble! We'll get that bunch of swine out of there! Later we can make apologies!

Hitler's ruthless determination succeeded—for the moment. On September 8, 1943, the day Italy surrendered to the Western Allies, German forces disarmed the Italian troops with scarcely a shot and occupied most of Italy. They halted the Allied drive up the Italian peninsula.

That was not all. By a daring air-borne operation Hitler succeeded in rescuing Mussolini. German glider troops landed on a mountaintop where the Italian dictator was being held prisoner by the new Italian government. They quickly freed him and flew him off to Germany.

Hitler's resolute action in Italy helped to restore his position and prestige. Elsewhere, though, his fortunes continued to decline. No amount of energy and will power could restore them. By midsummer, 1944, not only were the Russians approaching the German frontier from the East, but the German generals knew it was only a question of a few weeks before the Anglo-American armies under Eisenhower would be arriving at the German border from the West. To save the Fatherland from utter destruction some of the generals —but by no means all—decided that the time had come to get rid of Hitler.

Actually, a handful of army officers had made a number of attempts to kill their supreme warlord the year before—during 1943. Once on March 13 they had almost succeeded. On that day General Henning von Tresckow, Chief of Staff of Army Group Center on the Russian front, contrived to plant a time bomb in Hitler's airplane just before it took off following a visit of the Führer to the General's headquarters. But the mechanism failed and the bomb did not explode. A revolt in Berlin, which was timed by the generals to begin on receipt of the news of Hitler's death in a "plane accident," had to be hastily called off.

The plot was not abandoned. By midsummer of 1944 the anti-Nazi conspirators were again ready to strike. They realized that this might be their last chance. Time was running out.

On July 15, Field Marshal Rommel, who now commanded the main German armies trying to stem General Eisenhower's invasion forces in the

West, wrote Hitler: "The unequal struggle is nearing its end." He demanded that the warlord end the war "without delay."

Said Rommel to one of his generals that day: "I have given Hitler his last chance. If he does not take it, we will act."

Colonel von Stauffenberg, who was carrying in his bulging brief case the bomb to kill Hitler, belonged to one of Germany's most illustrious military families. A gifted staff officer, he was also a poet and musician. Now thirty-seven years old, he had been strikingly handsome until his staff car hit an American land mine in Tunisia the year before. In the explosion Stauffenberg lost his left eye, his right hand and two fingers of the other hand.

These mutilations made it difficult for him to handle the bomb he was confidently carrying. He had trained himself to set it off by using a pair of sugar tongs which he manipulated with the three fingers of his left hand.

The bomb, of English make, was identical to the one which General von Tresckow had planted in the Führer's airplane the year before. The ingenious weapon had no clock mechanism whose ticking could give it away. It emitted no sound at all when it was set off.

It worked as follows: First, a glass capsule was broken. The corrosive acid in the capsule then ate away a small wire. This released the firing pin against the percussion cap and the bomb went off.

The thickness of the wire governed the time required to set off the explosion. On this morning of July 20, 1944, Stauffenberg had fitted his bomb with the thinnest possible wire. When he broke the capsule with his tongs the wire would dissolve in ten minutes. The bomb would then explode. And that, the Colonel was sure, would be the end of Adolf Hitler.

Stauffenberg arrived by plane at Supreme Headquarters at Rastenburg in East Prussia shortly before noon on July 20, 1944. After conferring with Field Marshal Wilhelm Keitel, Chief of the Supreme Command, he excused himself for a moment. In an anteroom he hastily opened his brief case and with his tongs broke the capsule of the bomb.

The time was 12:32 P.M. In ten minutes there would be—if all went well—an explosion.

Hitler's midday military conference with his generals had already begun when Stauffenberg, accompanied by Keitel, arrived in the map room of the small wooden conference hall. The warlord was seated at the center of one side of a long table around which some two dozen officers stood. Stauffenberg took his place a few feet to one side of the Führer. He placed his brief case under the table against the *inner side* of a stout oaken support. It lay about six feet from Hitler's legs.

Hitler greeted the one-eyed, one-armed colonel curtly. He said he would hear his report as soon as one of the generals had finished his account of the situation on the Russian front. As the general resumed his report, Stauffenberg whispered to a Colonel Brandt, who was standing next to him, that he had to make an important telephone call. He slipped out of the room.

And now unwittingly Brandt made a fateful gesture. Finding that Stauffenberg's brief case blocked his feet when he leaned over the table to study the map, he bent down and removed it to the *far side* of the heavy table support. This heavy slab of oak now stood between the bomb and Hitler. Brandt's innocent gesture saved Hitler's life. It cost Brandt his own.

Time was now ticking away, though there was no telltale sound from the brief case.

Keitel, to his immense annoyance, had noticed the young colonel slipping out. He wondered why.

Finally he tiptoed out of the room to see. There was no trace of Stauffenberg. The telephone operator said the one-armed colonel with a patch over one eye had hurriedly left the building. Puzzled, Keitel returned to the map room. The general who was reporting on the Russian front was nearing the end of his account. Stauffenberg was due to report next on troop replacements. Keitel felt embarrassed by his unexplainable absence. But not for long.

At precisely 12:42 P.M. the bomb went off.

Stauffenberg, standing at a vantage point two hundred yards away, watched Hitler's conference hall go up with a roar of smoke and flame. It was as if, he said later, it had been directly hit by a 155 mm. shell. Bodies came hurtling out of the windows. Debris flew into the air.

There was not the slightest doubt in Stauffenberg's mind that every single person in the conference room was dead or dying. He bolted for the camp exits, bluffed his way past the guards, drove hastily to the nearby airport, climbed into his plane and was soon speeding back to Berlin. Having killed Hitler, as he thought, he must now lead the military revolt in Berlin.

But Stauffenberg had not succeeded in killing Hitler. The Führer was badly shaken but not severely injured. The oaken table support had saved his life. His hair was singed, his legs were burned, his right arm was bruised and temporarily paralyzed. His eardrums had been punctured by the force of the explosion and his back lacerated by a falling beam. But he was very much alive.

He was so much alive, in fact, that less than four hours later he was able to receive Mussolini, who had been invited to visit headquarters on this day of all days. Hitler showed his old Fascist comrade through the still smoldering debris where his life had almost been snuffed out.

I was standing here by this table [Hitler pointed]. The bomb went off just in front of my feet.

The Führer then drew a very typical conclusion.

It is obvious that nothing is going to happen to me. Undoubtedly it is my fate to continue on my way and bring my task to completion. . . .

In the excitement that followed the explosion, it was perhaps difficult for Hitler to remember how badly the war was going against him. But his mind was clear enough by teatime to provoke him into one of the most tumultuous rages of his life. By this hour—about 5:00 P.M.—communications with Berlin had been restored and the warlord learned that a military revolt had broken out in the capital and that there was another one among his generals in Paris.

Someone during tea recalled the alleged Roehm "plot" of June 30, 1934, which Hitler had suppressed so bloodily. Mention of this ignited the dictator like a match put to a firecracker. Eyewitnesses say he leaped from his chair, foam on his lips, and screamed and raged. What he had done to Roehm and his "treasonable followers" was nothing, he shouted, to what he would do to the traitors of this day. He would destroy them all, he cried. "I'll put their wives and children into concentration camps and show them no mercy!"

His revenge was made easier by the failure of the generals' revolt in both Berlin and Paris. Though it had been long and carefully prepared by some of the best military minds in the army, the revolt was unbelievably bungled. Stauffenberg, on his return to Berlin three hours after setting off the bomb, made heroic efforts to take over the capital and proclaim the Nazi regime dissolved. But the news that Hitler was still alive made most of the generals hesitate. By midnight the revolt had died down. Late that evening Stauffenberg himself was lined up against a wall of the War Ministry and shot by a firing squad.

At 1:00 A.M. on July 21, Hitler's somewhat hoarse and shaky voice burst upon the summer night's air in a nationwide broadcast from Supreme Headquarters. He told the German people that he wanted them to hear his voice so that they would know that "a crime unparalleled in German history" had failed.

A very small clique of ambitious, irresponsible, senseless and stupid officers concocted a plot to eliminate me. . . . The bomb planted by Colonel Count von Stauffenberg exploded two yards to the right of me. It seriously wounded a number of my true and loyal collaborators, one of whom has died. I myself am entirely unhurt, aside from some very minor scratches, bruises and burns. I regard this as a confirmation of the task imposed on me by Providence.

Hitler ended by promising that he "would settle accounts."

He kept his word. Thousands of suspects, military and civilian, were put to death. The surviving leaders of the conspiracy were tortured in prison to make them confess. Then they were given trials by the so-called "People's Court" and sentenced to death. Execution in many cases was carried out by slow strangulation while the victims were suspended by piano wire from meathooks borrowed from butcher shops.

Field Marshal von Witzleben was thus strangled. Field Marshals von Kluge and Rommel and General Beck managed to cheat Hitler of his cruel revenge by killing themselves. Rommel, because of his past services to the warlord, actually was offered by Hitler the choice of suicide or trial for treason. He preferred killing himself to being hanged.

This did not prevent Hitler from publicly announcing that the popular Rommel had died a "hero's death" as the result of his wounds in Normandy. The warlord sent the widow a wire:

"Accept my sincerest sympathy for the heavy loss you have suffered with the death of your husband."

Though he had escaped death by a miracle and had put down the generals' plot with his customary energy and brutality, Adolf Hitler was never the same after July 20, 1944. General Guderian, who now became Chief of the Army General Staff, later recalled the change.

What had been hardness became cruelty, while a tendency to bluff became plain dishonesty. He often lied without hesitation and assumed that others lied to him. He believe no one any more. It had already been difficult enough dealing with him. It now became a torture that grew steadily worse from month to month. He frequently lost all self-control and his language grew increasingly violent. In his intimate circle he found no restraining influence.

Nevertheless, it was this man alone, half-mad and rapidly crumbling in body and mind, who now rallied the beaten, retreating German armies and put new heart into the battered German nation, just as he had done in the grim, snowy winter of 1941 before Moscow.

By an incredible exercise of will power which all the others in Germany lacked—in the army, in the government and among the people—Adolf Hitler was able almost singlehandedly to prolong the agony of war for well nigh a year.

The Collapse of Hitler's Germany

At the end of August, 1944, barely six weeks after the bomb attempt against Hitler, the German generals concluded that the war was over and lost.

By the middle of that month the Russian summer offensive had carried the Red armies to the border of East Prussia, to the Vistula River opposite Warsaw, and well into the Balkans. By the end of August Hitler's remaining allies were lost. Finland gave up. Bulgaria withdrew from the war. Rumania, whose oil fields were Germany's only major source of natural oil, was overrun by the Russians.

In the West, General Eisenhower's armies captured Paris on August 25 and then raced toward the German frontier. In France alone the Germans had lost half a million men and most of their tanks, artillery and trucks. There was very little left with which to defend the Fatherland.

"As far as I was concerned," Field Marshal von Rundstedt, Commander in Chief in the West, said later, "the war ended in September."

Not for Adolf Hitler. On the last day of September the warlord attempted to revive the hopes of his generals.

If necessary [he said] we'll fight on the Rhine. It doesn't make any difference where. We will continue this battle until, as Frederick the Great said, one of our . . . enemies gets too tired to fight any more. I live only for the purpose of leading this fight. . . .

It was in this fighting mood that Hitler took his last desperate gamble of the war. He scraped up the last reserves in men, tanks and guns and ordered an offensive against the American front where it was weakest—in the Ardennes Forest on the border between Belgium and Germany.

The German generals were skeptical of success. They no longer had any confidence in their warlord's military judgment. They saw he was becoming a broken man. One of them later recalled his appearance on the night of December 12, 1944, when he gave the final order for the attack against the Americans.

Hitler was a stooped figure with a pale and puffy face. He sat hunched in his chair. His hands trembled. His left arm twitched. When he walked he dragged one leg behind him. A sick man . . .

Sick he may have looked. But his words were as fiery as ever. He urged his generals to give all they had. "A few more blows," he said, "and the Americans will be finished."

The blow Hitler's armies struck against the United States First Army in the hilly Ardennes Forest on the cold, snowy dawn of December 16, 1944, was a hard one. But it was not quite hard enough. Though the German breakthrough was swift and deep, the bulge it made was soon contained. By Christmas Day the Germans knew that Hitler's gamble had failed. The Battle of the Bulge, as it was called, was lost. By January 16, 1945, just a month after the launching of the surprise attack, Hitler's troops were back to the positions from which they had started.

Then the Russians struck in the East. They launched their greatest offensive of the war. They drove the Germans out of East Prussia. They cleared them out of Poland. By the end of January Marshal Zhukov, the top Soviet commander, was over the Oder River. His forces were now within one hundred miles of Berlin.

Most catastrophic of all for Hitler, the Russians had overrun the Silesian industrial basin near the Polish border. Germany's main mining and manufacturing region, the Ruhr in the West, already was largely in ruins from Anglo-American bombing. The loss of Silesia, which had escaped damage from bombing, doomed Hitler. He could no longer produce the weapons to continue the fight.

"The war is lost!" Albert Speer, the cool-headed chief of armament production, told the Führer on January 30, 1945, the twelfth anniversary of Hitler's coming to power. To prove it Speer gave the dictator the facts and figures. They showed that with Silesia gone and the Ruhr a mass of rubble, Germany simply could not continue to fight a war.

The terrible realization was at last beginning to dawn on the fanatical warlord. Typically, he put the blame on others.

If the German people are to be defeated in this struggle [he said], it must have been too weak. It has failed to prove its mettle before history and is destined only to destruction.

163

Adolf Hitler now willed this destruction himself.

He was fast becoming a physical and mental wreck, and this helped to poison his views. During September, 1944, he had suffered a breakdown and had been confined for several days to bed. He seemed to recover in November when the enemy on both the Eastern and Western fronts was temporarily halted. But he never recovered control of his terrible temper. Now in 1945, as each day brought disastrous news from the fronts, he gave way increasingly to hysterical outbursts.

General Guderian has described the warlord's tantrums on receipt of the news that the Red army had broken through at the end of January to the Oder River, only a hundred miles from Berlin.

His fists raised, his cheeks flushed with rage, his whole body trembling, the man stood in front of me. He was beside himself with fury, having lost all self-control . . . his eyes seemed to pop out of his head and the veins stood out in his temples.

In this state of mind and health, as his whole world began to crash down upon him, Adolf Hitler made one of the last momentous decisions of his life. On March 19, with the Russians and the

Western Allies closing in on the heart of Germany, he decreed the destruction of the land and people he had led to catastrophe. He ordered that all areas in Germany threatened by the advancing enemy be laid waste. Everything was to be destroyed—even the last stores of food and clothing. If he, the warlord, had to die, the German people must die with him.

Albert Speer, one of the few German officials who dared to stand up to the mad dictator, protested. He told Hitler he had no right to destroy the German people.

We must do everything [Speer insisted] to maintain, even if only in a most primitive manner, a basis for existence of the nation to the last.

But Hitler, now that his own personal fate was sealed, was not interested in the continued existence of the German people, for whom he had always professed such boundless love. Speer, on the stand at the Nuremberg Trials, quoted the warlord's answer.

If the war is lost [Hitler said], the nation will also perish. This fate is inevitable. There is no necessity to take into consideration the basis which the people will need to continue a most primitive existence.

165

On the contrary, it will be better to destroy these things ourselves because this nation will have proved to be the weaker one. And the future will belong solely to the stronger eastern nation [Russia]. Besides, those who will remain after the battle are only the inferior ones. For the good ones have been killed.

Hitler thereupon insisted on laying waste the German land. Millions of Germans, as well as foreign captives, would have perished had Hitler's orders been carried out. Fortunately, Speer and other German officials and army officers refused—finally!—to obey their dictator. And Allied and Soviet troops advanced so fast that even those fanatical Nazi officials who did try to obey had no time to destroy very much.

On the first day of April, 1945, the United States First and Ninth Armies completed their encirclement of the Ruhr, trapping twenty-one German divisions there. The road to Berlin lay open for Eisenhower's troops. On the evening of April 11 American contingents reached the Elbe River near Magdeburg, only sixty miles from the German capital.

On April 16 Zhukov's Russian armies broke

loose from their bridgeheads over the Oder River and converged on Berlin. They reached its outskirts on the afternoon of April 21.

The last days of Hitler had come.

The Death of Adolf Hitler

Hitler had planned to leave Berlin for Berchtesgaden on April 20, 1945, his fifty-sixth birthday. There from his villa on the Obersalzberg he intended to direct the last stand of the Third Reich. But he hesitated until it was too late.

Eva Braun, the blond Bavarian lady who had been Hitler's devoted friend for nearly thirteen years, had arrived in Berlin on April 15 to share his fate. Hitler had not seen much of her during the five and a half years of war. He had refused to allow her to visit him at his various headquarters where he had spent most of the war years. She had remained behind at the Villa Berghof on the Obersalzberg.

"She was," said Erich Kempka, the Führer's chauffeur, "the unhappiest woman in Germany. She spent most of her life waiting for Hitler."

The Führer's birthday on April 20 passed quietly enough despite the continued bad news from the collapsing fronts. Most of the old-guard Nazis and surviving military commanders gathered to offer Hitler birthday congratulations. Among them were Goering, Goebbels, Himmler and Ribbentrop; also Admiral Karl Doenitz, Commander in Chief of the Navy, and Generals Keitel, Jodl and Krebs. (Krebs had succeeded Guderian as Chief of the Army General Staff.)

During his birthday celebration in the air raid shelter under the Chancellery in Berlin, Hitler seemed to the generals to be strangely confident. The Russians, who were now at the gates of the city, would somehow, he said, be thrown back. The next day Hitler ordered an all-out counterattack on the Russians in the southern suburbs by S.S. General Felix Steiner.

"Any commander who holds back his forces," the warlord thundered, "will forfeit his life in five hours!"

All through the day and far into the next, Hitler waited impatiently for news of Steiner's counterattack. It was a further example of his loss of contact with reality.

There was no Steiner attack. It was never attempted. It existed only in the feverish mind of the desperate warlord. When he was finally forced to recognize this, the storm broke.

The blowup came at 3:00 P.M. on April 22, 1945, at the military conference in the underground bunker of the Chancellery, which now served as the Führer's headquarters. Hitler angrily demanded news of Steiner. Neither the generals nor anyone else had any. But the generals had other news. Russian tanks had broken through in the north and were now within the city limits of Berlin.

All the surviving witnesses testify that Hitler completely lost control of himself. He flew into the greatest rage of his life. This was the end! he shrieked. Everyone had deserted him. He was surrounded by treason, lies, corruption and cowardice. All was over. When he finally got control of himself he announced that he would stay in Berlin, and there meet his end. He summoned a secretary and dictated a brief statement to be read on the radio. The Führer, it stated, would remain in the capital and defend it to the last.

That evening he ordered Generals Keitel and Jodl, his faithful lackeys on the Supreme Command throughout the war, to leave the city and proceed to the south to take over command of the remaining German forces there. When Jodl protested that the warlord could not "lead anything" from Berlin, Hitler retorted: "Well, then, Goering can take over the leadership down there." The generals told him that "no soldier would fight for Goering."

"What do you mean, fight?" Hitler sneered. "There's precious little more fighting to be done!"

At long last Adolf Hitler finally admitted that the end had come. He knew that the Russians and Americans were nearing a junction on the Elbe River which in a day or two would slice Germany in two and cut him off in Berlin.

We have a firsthand picture of Hitler that stormy evening on April 22 from a zealous S.S. officer named Gottlob Berger. This individual arrived in the bunker late that evening. He later said he found Hitler "a broken man—finished." When Berger ventured to praise the Führer for remaining in Berlin and not deserting his people "after they had held out so loyally and long," Hitler shrieked at him: "Everyone has deceived me! No one has told me the truth!"

He went on and on [Berger later recounted] in a loud voice. Then his face went bluish-purple. I thought he was going to have a stroke any minute ...

Berger was flying south to Munich that night to take charge of a number of distinguished prisoners such as Dr. Schuschnigg, the former Austrian chancellor, Leon Blum, the former premier of France, and General Halder, the former Chief of the German General Staff. He was also to stamp out uprisings which had been reported in Bavaria and Austria. The idea that revolt could break out in his native Austria and adopted Bavaria once more convulsed Hitler.

His hand was shaking [Berger later said], his leg was shaking and his head was shaking. And he kept shouting: "Shoot them all! Shoot them all!"

Whether that meant to shoot both the distinguished prisoners and the rebels, Berger did not know. At any rate, he never got the chance.

Later that evening of April 22 General Eckard Christian, an air force liaison officer in the bunker, telephoned his Chief of Staff excitedly: "The Führer has broken down!"

The top man in the air force, Reich Marshal Goering, provoked a further breakdown the next day. Goering, like Himmler and Ribbentrop, had slipped out of Berlin the night of Hitler's birthday. None of these prominent Nazis wanted to be captured by the Russians. Goering set himself up at Berchtesgaden. From there on April 23 he sent Hitler a radiogram suggesting that since the Führer was now cut off in Berlin he, Goering, should take over the rule in Germany. This had been agreed to earlier by Hitler in case he were incapacitated. Goering added that if no reply was received that night, he would judge the Führer "incapacitated" and would take over.

Hitler's outburst when he received this message was later described by Nazi eyewitnesses.

Goering has betrayed and deserted both me and the Fatherland! [Hitler stormed]. Behind my back he has established contact with the enemy! Against my orders he has gone to save himself at Berchtesgaden. From there he sent me a . . .

At this point Hitler was so beside himself with rage that he could not go on. Finally he blurted out:

. . . sent me . . . a crass ultimatum! Now nothing remains! Nothing is spared me! No allegiances are kept, no honor!

Hitler immediately ordered Goering arrested as a traitor and expelled from all his party and government offices. The corpulent air force chief actually had not been in contact with the enemy, as the raving dictator charged. But another of Hitler's most trusted party followers had been. This was Heinrich Himmler, chief of the Gestapo. "The true and loyal Heinrich," Hitler had often called him.

On the very evening that Goering was radioing Hitler—April 23—Himmler had conferred secretly at Luebeck with Count Folke Bernadotte of Sweden. He had offered to surrender the German armies in the West. The news soon leaked out. Hitler heard it from a British broadcast from London on the night of April 28.

The Führer, one eyewitness in the bunker later testified, "raged like a madman. His color rose to a heated red. His face was virtually unrecognizable. Then he sank into a stupor."

The shattering news of Himmler's "treachery" was followed immediately by reports that the Russians were nearing the Chancellery. The realization that within thirty-six hours or so they would storm his underground headquarters seems to have cleared Hitler's mind.

He now took the last decisions of his life. By

dawn of the next day, April 29, he had ordered the arrest of Himmler, married Eva Braun, drawn up his last will and testament and decided on the time and the manner in which he and his bride would depart this earth.

Goebbels rounded up an obscure city councilor who was fighting on the barricades not far away. Sometime between 1:00 A.M. and 3:00 A.M. this official pronounced the Führer and Eva Braun man and wife in a brief civil ceremony.

A macabre wedding breakfast followed in Hitler's small private apartment in the underground bunker. Champagne was brought out and the falling dictator reminisced with his old Nazi cronies about happier times. Then, according to eyewitnesses, Hitler launched into a long review of his dramatic life. That life, he concluded, was now ended and it would be a release for him to die. Talk of his death plunged the wedding party into gloom. Some of the guests stole away in tears. Hitler himself slipped out. In an adjoining room he began to dictate to one of his women secretaries his last will and testament.

The document survives, as Hitler intended it to. It is interesting because it reveals the thoughts and the character of the Nazi dictator in the last hours of his stormy life. In those final moments he confirmed how little he had learned despite all his experience.

He cursed the Jews for all the ills of the earth. He whined that Fate once more had cheated Germany of victory and conquest. And he spewed forth the same old shabby lies that had marked his meteoric path through life. His last will and testament, in fact, is a fitting epitaph of a power-drunk tyrant whom absolute power had corrupted absolutely.

. . . It is untrue [he wrote] that I or anyone else in Germany wanted war in 1939. It was provoked exclusively by those statesmen who either were Jewish or worked for Jewish interests . . .

Having blamed the Jews for starting the war, he placed on them "sole responsibility" not only for all the millions of deaths on the battlefields and in the bombed towns but for his own massacre of millions of Jews! He then turned to the reasons for his decision to remain in Berlin to the last.

I cannot forsake the city that is the capital of this state. . . . I wish to share my fate with that which millions of others have also taken upon themselves by remaining in this town. I shall not fall into the hands of the enemy, who requires a new spectacle presented by the Jews to divert their hysterical masses.

I have therefore decided to remain in Berlin and there to choose death voluntarily at that moment when I believe that the position of the Führer can no longer be maintained. I die with a joyful heart in my knowledge of the immeasurable deeds and achievements of our peasants and workers and of a contribution unique in history of our youth which bears my name . . .*

With that the supreme German warlord was finished. It was now 4:00 A.M. on Sunday, April 29, 1945. Hitler called in four officials to witness the document and affix their signatures. He then quickly dictated a personal will in which he explained the reasons for his last-minute marriage and for the manner of his proposed death.

Although during the years of struggle I believed that I could not undertake the responsibility of marriage, now, before the end of my life, I have decided to take as my wife the woman who, after many years of true friendship, came to this city, already almost besieged, of her own free will to share my fate.

She will go to her death with me at her own wish as my wife. . . . My wife and I choose to die in order to escape the shame of overthrow or capitulation. It is our

---

* He refers to the so-called "Hitler Youth."

wish that our bodies be burned immediately in the place where I have performed the greater part of my daily work during the twelve years of service to my people.

Exhausted by the dictation of his farewell messages, Hitler went to bed as dawn was breaking over Berlin on this last Sabbath of his life. A pall of smoke hung over the city. The walls of the Chancellery above the bunker crashed in flames as the Russians began to fire point-blank into them. Probably Adolf Hitler did not get much sleep.

During the afternoon of April 29 one of the last pieces of news from the outside world to reach Hitler in the shelter came in by radio. Mussolini, who had returned to Italy, had met his end. It, too, had been shared by his mistress, Clara Petacci. They had been caught by Italian partisans on April 26 while trying to escape from northern Italy into Switzerland and had been executed two days later.

On the Saturday night of April 28 their bodies were brought to Milan in a truck and dumped on the Piazza. The next day they were strung up by the heels from lampposts and later cut down. The rest of the Sabbath they lay in the gutter, where vengeful Italians reviled them.

It is not known how many of the details of Mussolini's shabby end were communicated to the Führer. One can only speculate that if he heard many of them he was strengthened in his resolve not to allow himself and his bride to be similarly treated.

On the evening of April 29, Hitler instructed a secretary to destroy his remaining papers. For several hours he remained in his private quarters with Eva Braun.

At 2:30 A.M. of April 30 he emerged alone and bid farewell to several members of his entourage. He walked down the line shaking hands with each and mumbling a few words that were inaudible. There was a heavy film of moisture in his eyes. One of his women secretaries later remembered that his eyes "seemed to be looking far away, beyond the walls of the bunker."

Most of the people in the shelter expected that Hitler would commit the final act of his life before daybreak. But he waited.

At noon on April 30 he held his usual midday military conference, the last that was ever to take place. The news was such that he could no longer procrastinate. The Russians, he was told, had broken into the Potsdamerplatz, just a block away. It was a question of only hours before they would storm the Chancellery.

At 2:30 P.M. Erich Kempka, the Führer's chauffeur, who was in charge of the Chancellery garage, received an order to deliver immediately fifty gallons of gasoline in jerricans to the garden above. While the oil to provide the fire for the Viking funeral was being collected, Hitler and his bride bid their final farewells to the inner circle: Dr. Goebbels, Martin Bormann, the party secretary, two women secretaries and the generals, Krebs and Burgdorf.

Frau Goebbels did not appear. She was fighting in the loneliness of her small room for the strength, as she told someone, to kill her six young children before she and her husband ended their own lives. This was done the following day.

Hitler and Eva Braun had no such problems. They had only their own lives to take. They finished their farewells and retired to their rooms.

Outside in the passageway, Dr. Goebbels, Bormann and a few other faithful followers waited. In a few moments one revolver shot was heard. They waited for a second shot, but there was only silence. After a decent interval they quietly entered the Führer's quarters.

They found the body of Adolf Hitler sprawled on the sofa dripping blood. He had shot himself in the mouth. At his side lay Eva Braun. Two revolvers had tumbled onto the floor, but the bride had not used hers. She had swallowed poison.

It was 3:30 P.M. on Monday, April 30, 1945— ten days after Adolf Hitler's fifty-sixth birthday. It was twelve years and three months to a day since the one-time Vienna tramp had become Chancellor of Germany and had established the so-called Third Reich.

The corpses were carried up to the garden and, during a lull in the bombardment, placed in a shell hole and ignited with gasoline. No remains were ever found. They were undoubtedly blown into a thousand pieces by the explosions of Russian artillery shells. Erich Kempka, the chauffeur, who fetched the gasoline, has testified to that.

The bones are gone. But the memory of Adolf Hitler remains. To most people, probably, he seems like a monstrous tyrant as one follows his bloodstained trail. But while he lived and conquered he did not seem like that to most Germans. They worshiped him and did his awful bidding.

The remembrance of the grisly world nightmare he provoked, of the millions of innocent beings he slaughtered, of the hurt he did to the human spirit, lingers on. The memory fades but slowly as the years pass and mankind resumes its ages-old effort to make the world a more decent place in which to live.

Index

185